DOWN THE ROAD

UNEMPLOYMENT AND THE FIGHT FOR THE RIGHT TO WORK

Text: Sarah Cox Photography and Design: Robert Golden

Writers and Readers Publishing Cooperative

Our thanks to the many people who agreed to be interviewed for this book and advised and helped us while it was in preparation, in particular to Ken Appelby and Jason Meyler for their interest and advice; to Tommy Douras, Carol Douras, Dave Hayes, Marcus Luck and Dave Neve for their hospitality and introductions; to Jenny Kane for transcribing tapes and reading the book at many stages, Ruth Petrie for editing, Mary Phillips for typing, Steve White for making prints of the photographs and Tom Sullivan for advising on design.

First published 1977 by The Writers and Readers Publishing Cooperative, 14 Talacre Rd. London NW5

Printed in Great Britain by Butler & Tanner Ltd., Frome and London.

Contents

Employment Office
TR
EMPLOYMENT OFFICE
28. LLOYDS AVENUE.
INDUSTRIAL SECTION.
The Employment Service Agency
28

1. WHY

In the mid-nineteen seventies, after twenty-five years of almost full employment, unemployment in Britain reached an official total of a million and a half, the highest level since the pre-war depression. In many areas and in many industries it struck suddenly. For the first time since the thirties, almost every worker had friends, neighbours or relations on the dole with no easy prospect of finding another job.

During the fifties and sixties the cycle of booms and slumps seemed to have been permanently evened out. This cycle had plagued every capitalist country since the beginning of the industrial revolution, and for many years economists and politicians have searched for ways of regulating these fluctuations in the economy. Those who in the fifties and sixties thought they had found a regulator for the economy and a means of ending unemployment have to admit that it no longer works.

In the earliest days of capitalism, economists believed that, left alone, the system would balance itself in a most elegant and satisfying way. The supply of goods would balance demand, and at the level at which they balanced, prices would be fixed. Exports would balance imports, and this balance would determine the amount of trade. The supply of labour would balance the demand for it, and the price of labour — wages — would be fixed at that point. The supply of capital would balance demand at a level which would give investors a 'fair reward for risking their money'.

These economists, known as the 'laissez-faire' (let-well-alone) school, believed that any interference with the free play of market forces would upset these delicate balances. The politicians who accepted this view therefore opposed any attempts to control prices as well as moves by workers to combine in Trade Unions and improve their working conditions. Even the early attempts to prevent the employment of small children in mines, mills and factories for sixteen hours a day were seen as unwarranted interference in the system.

However, before long it became clear that the capitalist system did not balance itself automatically, but went up and down from boom to slump like a switchback at a funfair. These fluctuations are built into the system, and employment inevitably fluctuates with them, with unemployment rising in the slumps.

George V docks in the heart of Liverpool — recently closed

Stockpiled raw materials

Dockers waiting for work — Hull

7

As early as 1848, in the COMMUNIST MANIFESTO, Marx and Engels described how this switchback-ride from crisis to crisis is built into the capitalist system. Marx analysed the system in great detail in CAPITAL, first published in 1867.

A simplified explanation of Marx's complex analysis is: under capitalism, those with money use it to buy factories, equip them and employ workers to make goods. The capitalists then sell the goods, fixing the price so that it covers their expenditure on wages and raw materials and repays the cost of plant — their capital. They then add an extra element — profit. Most of this profit is reinvested to produce more goods and so make more profit, and in this way capitalists aim to accumulate more and more profit.

The goods produced are put on sale, but their prices add up to more than the wages which have been paid out to the workers. So the workers cannot afford to buy all the goods which are available. The capitalists do not absorb the surplus because they are reinvesting their profit as new capital. The result is an apparent surplus of goods — not more goods than people need, but more than they can afford.

The manufacturers then have to decide either to sacrifice their profit by lowering prices so that the workers can afford to buy more goods, or to cut production. Usually they cut production, but then fewer goods are being produced, fewer workers are employed and the total amount paid in wages falls. This means that workers have even less money to spend on goods. Production is cut once more, putting more people out of work, and this process continues until manufacturers cannot cut back any further. They reduce their prices and a price-cutting war follows in which some firms are forced out of business. But because workers can now afford to buy more of the goods, the upturn begins. More workers are taken on to expand production again. They spend their wages, creating more jobs, and the upturn continues until the point of overproduction is reached again.

The price-cutting war puts continual pressure on manufacturers to trim their profit margins, and then to invest more so that they can recover their lost profits through increasing production. The result is that over the years the rate of profit which capitalists can expect from their investment tends to fall.

Marx also explained that unemployment is not just a result of the crises, but that it is essential to the accumulation of profit since the unemployed act as a 'reserve army of labour' outside the factory gates which helps employers to discipline the workers inside the factory and keep their wages down.

Capitalism, then, far from being an elegantly rational system, is essentially irrational. The competition which is essential to its working eventually forces many firms to the wall, resulting in an increasing concentration of capital into the hands of large companies.

Throughout the competitive manoeuvrings the needs of people are subordinated to the demands of profit.

The demand for the right to work represents a refusal to accept this subordination. It asserts that people's skills, ability and creativity cannot be discarded simply to suit the investors of capital. To Victorian employers, workers were 'hands' or 'operatives', regarded as no more than extensions of their machines. The demand for the right to work contradicts this view, and because unemployment is essential to the working of the capitalist system, raising this demand challenges the basis of the system itself.

For more than a hundred years, until 1940, boom followed slump and slump followed boom. Several years of prosperity with increasing production, expanding trade and mounting profit were followed by years in which production fell, profits were squeezed and unemployment mounted.

Economists and politicians racked their brains to explain this trade cycle, decide who was to blame, and find ways of regulating it.

In the depths of the depression of the 1930s, the economist J.M. Keynes made suggestions about how an upturn in the economy could be started. If the crisis was caused by more goods being produced than workers could afford to buy, some people should be paid for work which did not produce any saleable product. This could be work which was socially useful, like building and staffing more schools and hospitals, improving roads, parks and playgrounds. These workers would then have money to spend and employment would be provided for the workers who produced goods for them to buy. These workers in turn would spend their wages and so the effect of the public works would spread through the whole economy. In this way, Keynes suggested, public works could be used to regulate the economy.

In the United States, President F.D. Roosevelt's New Deal Programme put some of these ideas into practice, but in Britain the National Government was not prepared to go into the debt that would result if they borrowed to provide public works. Like most governments faced with an economic crisis, they were cutting every public service.

The unemployment of the thirties was brought to an end only by the Second World War. In times of war governments are prepared to borrow massively, and millions of people are employed either in the forces or in the munitions industry.

After the First World War, many soldiers came home to find that there were no jobs for them. Although there was a short post-war boom, it never provided full employment.

The period after the Second World War was dramatically different. The war was followed by the cold-war years which produced a situation of full employment. The armaments industry, especially in the United States, employed a vast number of people who were producing something that could not be consumed or used, only stockpiled. For instance in 1962 the arms industry took nearly 10% of the gross domestic product of the United States. The spending of those employed in the armaments industry acted as a Keynesian regulator on the economy, preventing the slump which would otherwise have followed the first period of post-war reconstruction.

The regulating effect was exported from the States by programmes of aid and trade through which governments were lent large sums of money to spend on American arms and goods. The United States came to dominate the economy of the non-communist world to such an extent that it was said, "When America sneezes, the World catches cold."

Now the arms industry has become less effective as a regulator because with modern technology it employs fewer and fewer people, although it continues to absorb vast amounts of capital which could otherwise be used to finance welfare services or productive industry.

The decline in effectiveness of the arms industry in regulating the economy came at the same time as a succession of world shortages of raw materials which accelerated the recession.

The present crisis is international, and levels of unemployment are even higher in the States and as high in West Germany and other European countries as they are in Britain. It is impossible to make exact comparisons since the figures are collected on a different basis in each country, and in European countries many migrant workers from Turkey, Algeria or Yugoslavia are simply sent home when there are no jobs, so do not figure in the statistics of the unemployed.

Although the crisis is international, the British government can only seek solutions within this country, and even then they can not apply these solutions freely, since the country is dependent on international finance and international trade.

In the heyday of the British Empire, this country was able to exploit the colonies to provide cheap raw materials for British industry. The Empire, and later the Commonwealth, also provided a captive market for goods produced in Britain.

With the dissolution of the Empire, as the former colonies won their independence and American capital spread its influence, Britain was forced to compete in the world market for raw materials, and to compete with every other manufacturing country for export markets.

At the same time, production throughout the world has become concentrated more and more in the hands of the multinational companies which cannot be controlled by any single government.

In spite of the stranglehold of the international situation, politicians of every party suggest that they have the answer to the economic ills which beset us.

2. POLITICIANS AND PROMISES

Those who take meat from the table
Teach contentment.
Those for whom the taxes are destined
Demand sacrifice.
Those who eat their fill speak to the hungry
Of wonderful times to come.
Those who lead the country into the abyss
Call ruling too difficult for ordinary men.

Bertolt Brecht.

Faced with a situation in which the regulator has blown a gasket, politicians tinker with a system whose workings they do not fully understand and of which they are not in control.

At the beginning of the 1970s Edward Heath's Conservative government relied on conventional monetary controls such as altering interest rates and hire purchase conditions to try and stem the crisis. They combined these controls with phase after phase of incomes restraint, attempting to shift the responsibility for the crisis onto the workers and make them pay for it. The Conservatives were defeated in this strategy when they took on the miners in the winter of 1973—4 and introduced the three-day week, hoping to divide and break the working class. Their bluff was called, and in the election that followed in February 1974 Labour was returned to office.

The Labour Party's election posters promised to 'Get Britain back to work' and Anthony Wedgwood Benn echoed the manifesto pledging "A fundamental and irreversible shift of power and wealth from the rich to the poor." Some Tories openly advocated the use of a pool of unemployed as a way of regulating the economy, but Labour was outspokenly opposed to the policy of creating unemployment in order to control inflation and restore the balance of payments.

In the House of Commons in November 1974, Denis Healey, the Chancellor of the Exchequer, said:

> *"The Tories propose that shortages in the shops should be dealt with by depressing demand and throwing one million people out of work. This is morally obscene."*

It was in that same month that Harold Wilson spoke to the luminaries of the City, at the Lord Mayor's Banquet. He called for sacrifice and a tightening of belts. The sacrifice he called for was not from the financiers who shared the banquet with him that night, but from the working people who were to accept the six pound pay limit and massive cuts in public expenditure.

In spite of the eager cooperation of the Trade Union leaders in introducing policies which cut their members' living standards, by January 1976, with Wilson still Prime Minister, and Denis Healey Chancellor of the Exchequer, unemployment officially topped one million, four hundred thousand. The level dropped very little in the months that followed and rose higher still six months later, by which time Wilson had handed over to Callaghan.

Long-range economic forecasts suggest that an unemployment level of at least one million — the level that Healey considered morally obscene — will persist until 1980 or beyond.

Politicians and their promises change little over the years. In 1931, Ramsay MacDonald formed his National Government. It was supposed to be a coalition of talents from all parties, so that everyone could work together to lift the country out of its crisis. The National Government went to the country, promising above all else an end to unemployment. A year later, unemployment reached three million, the highest point of those desperate years. The government cut wages, dole payments and every public service. They also introduced the means test which denied all benefit to large numbers of the unemployed.

In Walter Greenwood's novel of life in Salford at that time, LOVE ON THE DOLE, one of the characters says:

> ". . . Yaaa! an' the bloody liars at election said everythin'd be apple pie if National Gover'ment went back. Well, where are we?"

*Street corner
in the 1930s*

*Street corner
in the 1970s*

Whatever promises politicians make in opposition, they find that being in office is not the same as being in power. The economy is not theirs to control. The international bankers know how to put on the screws. They attach political conditions to the loans they make, and any small step out of line is followed by a run on the pound, as sterling is converted into other currencies. In order to get the cooperation of those who control capital, the Labour government is forced to follow Tory policies. With the help of the Trade Union leaders, they do this even more effectively than the Tories themselves. The City greeted Healey's 1976 budget with jubilation. This was the budget which introduced the 4½% package, to succeed the 1975 £6 limit on pay increases.

The Labour government, which came into office committed to improvements in welfare and social services that would increase the 'social wage', is cutting back on every single service more savagely than any government since the war. These cuts have been accepted as part of the 4½% package by the leaders of the Trade Union movement — leaders who were elected, like the government, to represent the interests of the working class.

The living standards of working people have been slashed both by wage restraint and by cuts in social services. These cuts will inevitably cause unemployment: they cause unemployment in productive industry because people can afford less, and they cause direct unemployment among building workers, hospital workers, teachers, social workers, and the employees of both central and local government.

Nevertheless, the government argues that cuts must be made and wages must be restrained in order that profits can rise, and more money be made available for investment in industry. Industry, it is argued, will then expand and create more jobs.

There is no doubt that the very low level of investment in British industry is among the causes of the country's economic problems. Furthermore, factories in this country are often old and badly adapted to the use being made of them. Too often out-dated machinery forces inefficient production methods. It needs constant maintenance and creates difficult and unpleasant working conditions.

But there is absolutely no guarantee that making more money available in profits will result in a higher level of investment. When the supply of money was increased and credit restrictions were eased in the sixties to help industrial expansion, the extra money was invested not in industry, but in property speculation. Empty office blocks and half-used shopping centres throughout our cities bear witness to that boom which contributed to rising inflation and pushed the price of property to fantastic heights.

Unoccupied shopping centre — Ipswich

Nor is there any guarantee that increased industrial investment will provide more jobs. As industries invest in more sophisticated machines they are able to cut the workforce. This is already happening, even with the present low level of investment.

Unemployment fluctuates with every recession and recovery but in recent years, with each recovery, fewer jobs have been retrieved than were lost in the preceding recession. Even when the economy recovers completely, employment does not. There is a steady trend towards increasing unemployment even during 'good' times for the economy.

In order to stimulate investment in the areas hardest hit by unemployment, one government scheme offers factories ready built, rent free for two years or with a 22% grant towards the purchase price. Further grants are offered to help pay removal costs and install plant and machinery.

These offers have had little effect. The parts of the country which before the war were described as 'derelict' or 'distressed' areas are now 'development areas' or 'areas for expansion'. The description changes, but the situation remains the same.

Tyneside street, 1976

When manufacturers do take advantage of these offers, they often use government grants to equip the factory for automated or semi-automated production, which provides few jobs. Most of these factories produce consumer goods, for which demand falls quickly when times are hard, so that manufacturers move in for a few years and then move out, leaving unemployment in the area unchanged or even higher than before. Skelmersdale, on Merseyside, is a new town with an industrial estate, planned to provide homes and jobs for workers rehoused from Liverpool's slums.

Here, in the late sixties, Thorns built a factory with government help to manufacture tubes for colour television. With Philips, Thorns dominates the television industry in Britain, and they hoped to cash in on the boom in sales and rentals which they expected when colour television became readily available. Pilkingtons built a factory nearby to make glass especially for these tubes. In 1973, the workers at the 'Skem' factory made a profit for Thorns of almost £2m, but by 1975 recession had reduced demand for colour television. Pilkingtons were losing money and ran down their factory, and rather than import glass Thorns decided to import completed tubes from Taiwan.

They closed a component factory in Hull which had been opened for only eighteen months, and 250 women joined the dole queues. Then they started to run down the workforce at Skelmersdale. When the factory shut down 1400 people lost their jobs in an area where almost every factory was closing or cutting down its workforce.

Thorns, however, were able to declare a profit of £3.4m for the first half of 1975.

In nearby Kirkby, which vies with Skelmersdale for the title of Britain's most depressed new town, stands another factory built with government help — the Fisher Bendix plant, which opened in 1961 as part of the British Motor Corporation. Here, a skilled and experienced workforce made motor components and other high-quality products including Moulton bicycles and Bendix washing machines. When BMC became part of British Leyland, the Chairman, Lord Stokes, decided to limit production within the combine to motor vehicles and components.

He started to hive off products to firms outside the combine, selling the right to make Moulton bicycles to Raleigh. Then the factory was sold, and a series of changes of ownership followed, with each new owner altering further sections of production to suit the needs of their firm. When

Thorns took over the factory, they transferred the manufacture of Bendix washing machines to one of their factories in Spain and prepared to move the other products out and close the factory. The workforce had had enough. In January 1972 they occupied the factory, demanding that it be kept open. Harold Wilson, as MP for the constituency, intervened and acted as intermediary in the sale of the firm to a property company, Clohurst, later IPD, headed by his friend Harold King. So many products had been sold off that now Fisher Bendix was making only radiators and orange juice. This limited production, unsuitable to the skills of the workforce and equipment of the factory, combined with inefficient management, led the firm to the brink of bankruptcy in 1974. The workers occupied once more and staged a work-in to defend their jobs against the receiver. With the help of Anthony Benn's Department of Trade and Industry, a cooperative was set up which survived until 1976.

The setting up of a cooperative represents a great victory. It preserves some of the workers' jobs and brings to an end the continual transfer of ownership in which the workforce are just pawns, changing their trade to suit each new owner.

But there are dangers. Because a cooperative is usually formed when a firm has deteriorated to the point where it faces closure, the workers who take over find themselves responsible for clearing up the mess made by the previous management.

They also face the task of proving that the factory is viable within the terms of capitalist industry. In order to maintain this viability, workers in a cooperative may find themselves negotiating the redundancies of their fellow workers.

The cooperative at the Norton Villiers Triumph motor cycle factory near Coventry went into production pledged to a higher output from fewer workers, with lower wages and greater flexibility between trades than under any previous management. A factory that once employed 1,750 is seeking to double its former output with a workforce of 800. How easy it is for employers in the area to point to such a cooperative as an example when their workers demand higher wages or better manning levels.

For the government, helping a cooperative offers a cheap alternative to nationalization.

Workers in occupation, with valuable plant under their control, are in a strong position to demand nationalization without compensation, making the government take on the responsibility for clearing up the previous management's muddle.

Nationalization, under a capitalist system, cannot provide the solution to the economic problems, but it is a significant step forward.

When Thorns decide to buy television tubes from Taiwan, and transfer the manufacture of washing machines to Spain, they give ammunition to those who call for import controls to help Britain out of her economic crisis.

The multinationals are prepared to back this call because they know that they are in a position to evade any controls which might inconvenience them, and they are glad to see the anger of workers whose jobs are threatened diverted against workers overseas instead of being directed against the employers who are sending them down the road.

In the summer of 1975 Courtaulds and the other major textile manufacturers willingly gave their employees the day off with full pay to travel to London and demand controls on textile imports, at the same time as they were expanding production in their factories in Europe. The truth is not that the British textile industry is declining and no longer profitable, but that there are more lucrative pickings to be made elsewhere. Courtaulds and the other textile giants are not on their last legs by any means — in 1974 Courtauld's pre-tax profits rose by 70% *in a single year,* reaching £116.3m, and in January 1976 the Sunday Times Business News predicted:

> *"There are good grounds for thinking that when demand gets stronger, Courtaulds will be able to operate at greater profitability than anyone else in Europe."*

The first effect of import controls is to export unemployment to workers abroad and to raise prices at home. After the Portuguese revolution in April 1974, many textile mills and clothing factories were taken over by the workers and run under workers' control. The British government imposed controls on the import of Portuguese textiles. The result is described by Rosario, a member of the Portuguese textile and clothing workers union:

> *"The bosses of the British textile companies are calling for stricter import controls against Portuguese textiles. Many English factories used to work with cloth imported from Portugal. Restricting the supply of imports affects workers in my country and workers here who no longer have raw materials to work with.*
>
> *Import controls have made many Portuguese firms bankrupt. Now the multinationals have taken them over. They are increasing their hold over the industry and they are in a stronger position to manipulate workers, in Portugal and all over Europe.*

Spanish seaman

*International workers' solidarity is the strongest weapon
we have against the bosses. They operate internationally,
we must do the same."*

British industry relies heavily on the import of raw materials and
components, and it is very likely that import controls would interfere
with this trade and hamper production. There is also a strong possibility
that the imposition of import controls would lead to reprisals by those
countries we sell our exports to, and exporting, as we are endlessly
reminded, is vital to our economic strength. Whatever the relevance of
these arguments, the overwhelming argument against import controls is
the one given by Rosario. Capitalism is international. The working class
can only organise against it by recognizing that the interests of workers
are international too. Far from crying out for import controls, British
workers need to forge links with workers in factories of the same
combine overseas, to organise collectively against their multinational
bosses.

*English
building
worker*

In order to lessen the effects on the economy of international trade fluctuations, politicians have tried altering the value of the pound.

In 1925, the then Chancellor of the Exchequer, Winston Churchill, at the insistence of the Bank of England, put the pound back onto the Gold Standard. Its value was fixed at an unrealistically high level, in an attempt to achieve stability.

In fact, it made British exports so expensive that employers attempted to cut wages to compensate. In this way, the return to the Gold Standard was among the causes of the miners' lockout and the General Strike which followed, and helped to precipitate the slump of the thirties.

Since the war, the pound has been devalued several times, allowed to float and finally to sink with sporadic efforts to prop it up. As the pound sinks, it is hoped that it will find a level which makes the price of our goods attractive to buyers abroad, enables exports to increase and brings about an increase of production and a consequent increase in employment. But because so many of the raw materials and components used to make goods in British factories are imported, the downward movement of the pound raises the price of many products: exports may become cheaper, but imports become more expensive.

Much of the food in the shops is imported, so the fall in the value of the pound raises prices in the shops. For several years, workers were able to win wage increases which covered the rise in the cost of living, but world raw material shortages in 1974 and 1975 pushed import prices up even higher and at the same time wage restraint policies made it impossible for workers to keep up with inflation. Their spending power fell, which meant that manufacturers could not sell as many goods on the home market, while the increase in exports, hoped for as a result of the fall in the pound, was prevented because other countries were feeling the effects of the international recession and cutting their spending.

This meant that demand fell off in the home market and abroad. Manufacturers first ran down stocks, and then cut production, sending workers down the road.

The upturn in the economy may bring about an increase in exports and in production for export, but many small firms have been pushed out of business during the downturn of the cycle, and the giant firms, the multinationals and even the nationalized industries have used the opportunity to rationalize so that they can increase production through the use of speed-up, overtime and shift work without taking on many more workers.

3. THE NUTS AND BOLTS – INDUSTRIAL UNEMPLOYMENT

The continuing process of takeovers and mergers by which fewer and fewer giant firms gain an increasing share in the ownership and control of industry raises the level of unemployment.

The giant multinational companies buy up firms in their industry, close some plants and cut back production in others. Work is moved to other factories in this country or overseas. Many workers are sent down the road, and those who are still employed are worked more intensively.

Engineering workshop during the working day – London docks

The textile industry is one in which this rationalization process can be seen in action. It is dominated by four giant firms — Courtaulds, Carrington Viyella (ICI), Coats-Patons and Tootal. These firms buy up mills in the traditional textile areas, taking over small firms at such a rate that workers often have no idea who their employer is.

Having bought up the mills, they close some, moving the most modern machinery into other mills where it can be worked more intensively. The mills may have been making a small profit, but the workers are led to believe that new management has been forced to close them by the decline in the industry or competition from imported textiles. The government assists the rationalization process by giving generous grants for modernization programmes.

Blackburn, a Lancashire cotton town, had around 220 mills in 1920. Now it has seven. In one of these mills machines and some of the workers are being moved in from other mills which have been closed. Only the fastest and most efficient workers are offered a transfer when their mill closes, but their efficiency is not rewarded by a pay rise; the piece-work rates are lower in the mill they have been moved to, so they must accept a cut in wages or unemployment.

Modernization does not necessarily bring improvements in working conditions. In this same mill, machines are being modified to prevent threads tangling so that they can be supervised by fewer operatives, but the installation of ventilation and dust-control equipment is having to wait.

Having closed twelve mills in four years, management are thinking of introducing a night shift in addition to the early and late day shifts traditionally worked in the mills. In this way, they are able to keep up production, using modern machines all round the clock, and economize on administration, heating and maintenance costs, regardless of the effect on workers' health and the number of jobs lost.

Courtaulds cut its labour force from 128,000 to 110,900 between 1972 and 1975 and in those years they made record profits.

The many unions in the textile industry have done little to oppose these closures and redundancies. In almost every case they have actually cooperated with management. They accept the story that the industry is in decline and have agreed to three-shift working where mills are modernized, as well as joining in the clamour for import controls, instead of fighting to protect their members' jobs, wages and working conditions at home. The smaller craft unions illegally exclude women and immigrants from membership and so from certain jobs, helping the employers to divide the workforce and keep wages low.

Shift work, which is on the increase as firms rationalize, is known to injure health and raise the accident rate. The change of working hours from week to week causes tiredness and lethargy and shiftworkers commonly suffer from ulcers, indigestion, constipation and irritability. Family and social life are badly affected and children suffer from having to be kept quiet while the parent who has been working nights sleeps in the day time.

A survey at Vauxhall's Luton factory showed that accidents are more common on night shifts when fatigue undermines workers' concentration and dexterity, yet it is unusual to find the same medical care available to workers on nights as there is during the day.

A young engineering worker from Gloucester said, "I became unemployed basically because I was on permanent nights for eighteen months and I was feeling old at the age of 23." Failing to get a transfer to day work, he gave up his job and moved to Cardiff to search for another, but with no success.

In the mines, too, shift work is on the increase. Modern coal-cutting machinery has led to much higher productivity often at the expense of the miners' health, since dust levels at the coalface are higher than with older, slower methods of production. The machinery is expensive and the Coal Board, even though it has been making a profit since the wage increase won after the miners' strike made it possible to recruit enough miners to raise production, is anxious to extend the continental shift system. Under this system, machines can be kept running twenty-four hours a day, seven days a week. In the pits it means that there are four shifts in the twenty-four hours. Each worker does five days on one shift, has one or two days off, and then does five days on another shift.

This system is even more destructive of health and family life than a straight three-shift system where at least everyone has the same weekends off. It is also destructive of community life and union organization.

An unemployed miner from the Derbyshire area describes the effect of the system on the life of his village:

"The traditional cycle of operations in a pit is days, afters and nights. Now, that sets a traditional social and political pattern within that community. Today there are twenty-seven different shifts and so you've got a bigger break-up of community in social terms."

Hospitals, fire services and other essential services are needed day and night, so shift work is unavoidable for workers in these services, but in many productive industries shift work is introduced not to protect life or safety, but in the interests of profit. Then the demands of the machines are put before the needs of the workers.

Where shift work is already in operation or its introduction cannot be resisted, workers should demand that arrangements be made for the workers on every shift to meet together in the firm's time, so that union organization is not undermined by the fragmentation of the workforce into various shifts.

32

Where shift work is not in operation, overtime is increasing. So much overtime is worked in industry that to ban it would almost eliminate unemployment. The table below shows the amount of overtime worked in the manufacturing industries during a single week in December 1975. The figures were given in the House of Commons in March 1976. The second column divides the total number of hours by 40 to show how many jobs would be created if workers were taken on to do the work now done as overtime, and the third column shows the number of workers unemployed in each industry at the same date.

	Hours of overtime week-ended 13th December	Column (1) divided by 40	Unemployed December 1975
	(1)	(2)	(3)
Food, drink and tobacco	1,933,600	48,300	35,756
Coal and petroleum products	89,300	2,200	2,258
Chemicals and allied industries	617,900	15,400	15,002
Metal manufacture	1,086,200	27,200	23,756
Mechanical engineering	2,360,400	59,000	39,754
Instrument engineering	214,700	5,400	4,368
Electrical engineering	1,004,500	25,100	27,017
Shipbuilding and marine engineering ...	713,100	17,800	8,280
Vehicles	1,451,400	36,300	27,060
Metal goods not elsewhere specified ...	1,123,400	28,100	35,923
Textiles	702,700	17,600	26,300
Leather, leather goods and fur	75,900	1,900	3,538
Clothing and footwear	121,300	3,000	16,286
Bricks, pottery, glass, cement, etc. ...	716,000	17,900	13,671
Timber, furniture, etc.	593,800	14,800	13,283
Paper, printing and publishing	951,600	23,800	18,725
Other manufacturing industries	629,500	15,700	16,673
Total, all manufacturing industries	14,385,400	359,600	327,650

These figures relate only to manufacturing. Some of the service industries rely even more heavily on overtime. Bus services throughout the country depend on drivers and conductors working their rest days. On the railways, a 56-hour week is normal, while overtime in the hospital service is appalling. Junior doctors frequently work 80—100 hours a week, and hospital staff in record departments or laboratories regularly work a full day, a night and the following day — 32 hours on end — with no time off to compensate. Yet a mistake by any of these workers could cost a life.

Employers find it cheaper to rely on overtime than to take on more workers. As well as saving National Insurance contributions, they gain flexibility since overtime can be varied from week to week or department to department. For the employers it is cheaper, but for workers it means fatigue and a strain on family life.

5 p.m., railway workers waiting for their shift to begin

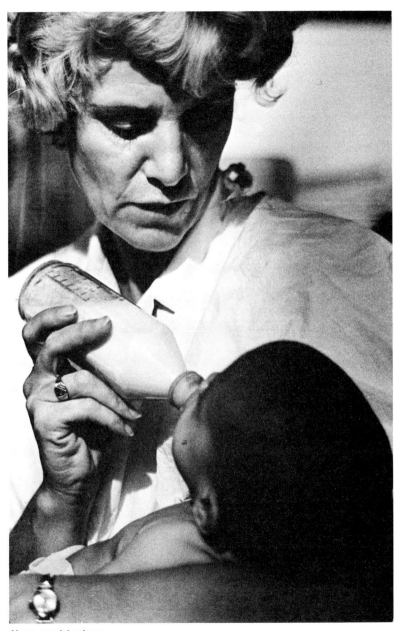

Nurse on night duty

A North West London engineering worker's wife said:

> *"When my husband was made redundant from the engineering factory where he was working, he found a maintenance job on the railway. He really enjoys the work, but one condition of the job was compulsory rostered overtime. He had to work every other weekend so that he worked twelve days without a break. He became really exhausted. I've never known him to have so much illness. The children missed him too, especially the younger one. She became really depressed. He used to take her out a lot at weekends, but with the overtime he'd had to stop.*
>
> *Now, with so much unemployment, he's said he will only do overtime in emergencies. His health has been much better since he has been working a normal week, and our little girl is far happier."*

But in many situations low wages force workers to accept overtime. A woman in a Lancashire cotton mill had worked from six in the morning until two. Her eyes were red from the dust, her ankles swollen from hours, weeks, years of standing, but she was about to start work on the second shift from two until ten at night. "It's the only way to make up the wages."

While low wages force workers to do overtime, overtime also keeps wages low, and divides workers. Foremen can use overtime to bribe workers, and union organization is undermined by quarrels over who is to work it. A miner from a very modern Yorkshire pit:

"There are so many quarrels about overtime. It divides the men here. This is not a militant pit. Where I came from, in Durham, we never worked overtime, and it shocked me when I came here to see the overtime that's worked. There's less solidarity here than we had in the pits back home."

Workers who can make up their money by working overtime are less ready to fight for higher basic rates, and too busy to consider how they are damaging their fellow workers.

An old Glasgow song describes someone most workers will recognise:

Three nights and a Sunday double-time,
Three nights and a Sunday double-time,
I work all day and I work all night,
To hell with ye Jack, I'm all right,
Three nights and a Sunday double-time.

There's a fellow down the road that I avoid,
He's one of them they call the unemployed.
He says it's all because of me,
He can't get a job when I've got three,
Three nights and a Sunday double-time.

Three nights and a Sunday double-time,
I work all day and I work all night,
To hell with ye Jack, I'm all right,
Three nights and a Sunday double-time.

The fight against overtime is part of the fight against unemployment. Between the wars the National Unemployed Workers' Movement led this fight. Wal Hannington, one of their leaders, describes in his book UNEMPLOYED STRUGGLES one of the raids carried out by members of the movement on factories where overtime was being worked.

In 1921, soon after the formation of the NUWM, members heard that an aircraft factory in Kilburn was working overtime. Thirty unemployed men from the Willesden branch gathered near the factory gates, some carrying football gear to dispel suspicion. They entered the factory, manned every exit, took over the telephones and shut off the machines. Hannington jumped onto a bench and called all the workers round him:

> *"I spoke briefly on the question of unemployment, the need for all overtime being stopped, and urged workers to realise that we, the organized unemployed, would be with them in any fight to prevent any reduction in their wage rates. While I was speaking, the manager came up, listened for a time to what I had to say, and then demanded that he also put his side of the case."*

Somehow, word of the raid had reached the police,

> *"But by the time the police arrived in the machine-shop I had finished speaking and the manager was now up on the bench haranguing the workers. A burly sergeant of the police marched in at the head of a dozen constables and to the amusement of the workers and the raiders, without waiting to grasp the actual situation, he rushed the manager, evidently taking him for the leader of the raid, and began to drag him down from the bench. He in fact succeeded in doing so before the manager — in a state of utter confusion — could acquaint the sergeant with the fact that he was the manager.*
>
> *The whole incident became a huge joke, the manager and the sergeant looked in a condition of utter bewilderment, while the crowd of workers and raiders roared with laughter."*

The manager agreed to negotiate with a few of the raiders and undertook to stop the overtime in the factory.

NUWM meeting, Trafalgar Square, 1932

Other raids followed, carried out by various branches of the NUWM in the London area, but this one was hard to equal for the audacity and imagination with which it was conceived and carried out.

The resistance to overtime as part of the fight against unemployment continues.

In March 1976, at International Harvesters in Doncaster, workers agreed not to accept the overtime they were offered, and were told that thirty more workers were being taken on the next day.

At Willesden College of Technology, lecturers who had been working overtime decided to stop. This was in the summer of 1976 when newly-trained lecturers were leaving college for the dole queue. The college authorities engaged thirty-two extra staff for the following term.

As well as increasing the use of overtime, shift work and new machines, all of which speed up the production process, managements call for greater flexibility from their workers. They claim that for workers to insist on sticking to the trade for which they were trained or the job they are used to doing is old-fashioned and leads to over-manning. Press and television point to the greater productivity of continental workers, especially those in Germany who work more flexibly, each worker covering a number of different jobs. The greater flexibility of workers in German industry, and the far greater use of the continental shift system means that unemployment levels are higher there than in Britain. It also means a sacrifice of health and safety that many British workers are not prepared to accept. It is not possible to compare accident rates in the two countries, but a group of workers and managers visiting German factories were deeply shocked by the neglect of safety precautions that would be taken for granted here.

Like shift working, 'flexibility' can lead to accidents. Workers are more likely to make mistakes when they are doing jobs for which neither their training nor their experience has prepared them.

In the steel industry, where 44,000 jobs are threatened, greater flexibility is called for to increase productivity and therefore profit, but it is only too easy to imagine the dangers that would be faced by workers doing jobs unfamiliar to them when they are handling hundreds of tons of molten steel.

Speed-up and flexibility can be resisted by non-cooperation tactics and an insistence on shopfloor control of the number of workers in each department.

In car factories where the line has been speeded up or the number of workers cut by, say, one sixth in the door-hanging section, it is not unknown for one car in six to come off the line without doors.

In 1975 the workers in a Merseyside printing factory had successfully resisted the threat of a hundred redundancies and kept the workforce intact. Then the management brought in more machines and redeployed the workforce to rationalize production. In one department this meant that machines which had formerly been worked by five women were to be worked by three. With the confidence gained from their previous victory, the women employed a tactic which the Mother of the Chapel described as 'organized chaos' to prove that three women could not do the work. Plastic containers were spraying out of the machines onto the floor because there were no boxes ready for them. The containers had to be scrapped and fed back through the extruder, and production fell drastically. Management called the stewards together and accused them of being 'quite unreasonable'. They were sure three women could manage the machines.

The stewards invited the management to try for themselves and show that it could be done. Management 'exploded'. The final result was a partial victory — one extra worker was put onto each machine.

In order to counter workers' resistance to rationalization or redundancies, giant companies with factories all over the country or throughout the world can transfer costs from one factory to another and produce figures to show that a particular factory is making a loss.

Walls is part of the Unilever combine. In 1976, they closed their modern meat and pie factory on the Park Royal estate in North West London, sending 1,600 workers down the road. They claimed that the factory was making a loss, but workers there learned that the sausage skins they were using, manufactured by other Unilever firms, were being sold to Walls at a higher price than was being asked from firms outside the Unilever group. Unilever made no loss on them, but Walls did.

This closure was yet another in an area which was once a major centre of engineering, railway work and the food industry. In the last ten years, ten thousand jobs have been lost on the Park Royal estate. Unemployment in the area rose by 83% between July 1975 and July 1976, and almost every other factory stands empty with FOR SALE or TO LET signs up and padlocks on the gates. Many of these factories are falling into complete decay.

There are a hundred ways in which a combine can use its monopoly position and the variety of its production to ensure that one of its companies makes a loss when it suits them to close it or enforce redundancies.

Multinational combines can transfer profit or loss from one country to another through the prices they charge their factories in one country for components made in one of their factories elsewhere. Taxes are high in Britain so companies find it convenient to make apparent losses or low profits here in order to make higher profits in countries where taxes are lower.

Chrysler UK, part of the giant American motor combine, propped up with £162m of government funds in Britain, was selling knockdown kits at a loss to a Swiss subsidiary. These were assembled in Switzerland and then sold at the full market price.

Multinationals can shift their operations across national boundaries and preserve their profits by taking advantage of concessions offered by various governments. Those who lose out are the workers, every time.

Statue of Henry Ford, Dagenham

The actions of the multinationals and the giant combines cause closures and redundancies among small, independent firms. When money is tight, the large corporations find it easy to press those firms which owe them money to pay up promptly. At the same time, the giants put off paying the firms which supply them, and keep them waiting for six months or more. Many of these suppliers depend for their existence solely on the major firm. They may have turned over all their production to fulfil a contract from the firm, and fear that if they insist on being paid, the firm will turn to another supplier, forcing them into bankruptcy. It is not uncommon for big firms to switch their suppliers in this way. And for every major redundancy or closure which attracts national publicity there are hundreds of smaller firms closing and laying off workers, each one sending a dozen more down the road and adding to the number of unemployed.

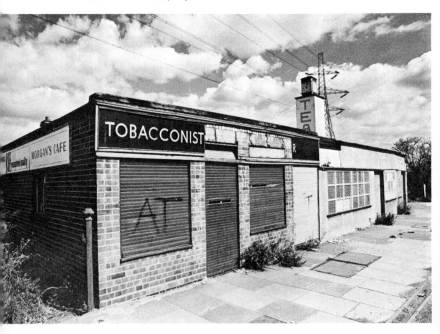

In areas where unemployment is rising and more and more people have to rely on the dole there is less money to spend. Shops begin to stock a smaller range of goods. This affects the firms producing consumer goods which in their turn lay off workers.

Local shops close down, each throwing a handful of workers onto the dole queue and adding to the desolation and decay of working class districts.

These are the areas, too, which are hardest hit by the cuts in the welfare services and community facilities.

Liverpool

4. WASTE—THE CUTS

My granny tells me that she's seen it all before
And at 94 she's seen a thing or two.
She's seen the stockbrokers all sighing
And the speculators crying
And the millionaires relying
On a war to pull them through. ·

And they're turning the clock back
I can hear my granny say,
Yes, they're turning the clock back,
And the working man will pay.

My granny tells me that they're at it once again.
The nobs can't get their profits quite as high,
And Tom and Dick and Harry
Have forgotten that they carry
On their shoulders all the parasites
That suck their bodies dry.

And they're turning the clock back
I can hear my granny say.
They may call it Social Contract
But the working man will pay.

Alex Glasgow.

Conservatives believe in free enterprise and a system where access to health care, welfare and education depend on one's ability to pay. For them it makes sense to cut public expenditure, and when Anthony Barber was Chancellor in the 1970—74 government they brought in massive cuts.

The Labour Party, on the other hand, is pledged to the belief that everyone has an equal right to a home, a free and decent education, and good health care. Before the two elections in 1974, they promised to restore the cuts made by the previous Tory government and to improve welfare services as part of the Social Contract. They recognized that it is not only wages, but all these services too which determine workers' living standards. Yet since they won those elections, each succeeding Labour budget has introduced new cuts in social services, and new limits on the spending of local authorities. Every one of the services on which the quality of workers' lives depends has been slashed so that the government can make more money available to industry to increase its profitability.

Thousands of tons of bricks stand stockpiled in the brickyards and building workers line up outside the dole. While more than 200,000 building workers are registered as unemployed, there are many more who were formerly working as self-employed sub-contractors now also unable to find work.

Council housing, new hospitals and schools were planned. One by one the projects are abandoned, but the need does not disappear. Hundreds of thousands of people are homeless, others still live in slums, and the slums deteriorate further. Patients still wait for hospital beds or are treated in wards so ancient that it is impossible to keep them clean. Children cram into old and dingy classrooms and pour out to play on asphalt playgrounds, catching the hopelessness of their decaying environment.

New building schemes are cut, maintenance work is slowed down. Councils cut their staff, delay repairs and decoration; the fabric of the neglected building decays. And more building workers are sent down the road.

New Council estates which were designed as cheaply as possible turn into slums when they are not maintained, and within the high-rise blocks frustration grows. Lifts break down, marooning the elderly twenty floors up, forcing young mothers to climb fifteen flights of stairs, dragging shopping bags, pushchair, baby and screaming toddler.

Vandalism increases. Young kids feel there is no harm in adding to the ugliness around them, school leavers, rejected by the adult world of work, vent their frustrations on their surroundings. Anyway, what else is there for them to do? Clubs and playcentres close or cut their staff and opening hours, playground apparatus, no longer maintained for reasons of economy, becomes dangerous and unusable, and swimming pools raise their charges. There is nowhere to go, nothing to do. With parents out of work or hard-pressed by rising rents and prices, there is no money for the kids.

Transport too is affected. Fares rise higher and higher, but the services are cut. Queues grow at the bus stops, trains are cancelled. London Transport pleads staff shortages, while people who apply to them for work are turned away. It is the conductors who have to face the anger of each waiting queue. Attacks on bus crews are increasing, and they have had enough. In London, in the summer of 1976 busmen went on strike to oppose further cuts in services, and many of the proposed cuts have been prevented.

In the schools, the first cuts were in equipment and the maintenance of buildings, now there are cuts in the number of teachers. The improvements in class size and conditions in school have been halted, and the slide backwards has begun. Classes will get larger; standards will fall.

Faced with the prospect of finishing a three-year training only to join the dole queue, student teachers decided in the summer of 1976 to take action and occupy their colleges in protest against the cuts and teachers' unemployment. The action spread from Scotland to almost every college in Britain. Students used the occupations as a springboard to go out and tell parents what the cuts would mean for their children's education, and to go into schools to persuade teachers that they should not cover classes for non-appointed or absent colleagues when there were so many teachers on the dole.

For years, parents and teachers have asked for smaller classes, more nursery education and more help for children with special needs. For years they have been told that authorities would love to provide all this, but there were not the teachers. Now the teachers are there, down at the dole, but the smaller classes, nurseries and special groups are as far away as ever.

If the Labour government were to implement its party's policy of bringing the size of classes down to thirty, 58,000 more teachers would be needed, according to Fred Mulley, Secretary of State for Education. There are about 30,000 teachers on the dole. Classes of thirty would mean another teacher shortage.

Although the students' training did not qualify them for any job other than teaching, they do not see themselves as a special case with more right to a job than anyone else: they see their struggle as part of the fight of all workers for the right to a job.

While all education services suffer from the cuts, nursery education, at one end, and colleges of further education at the other are hardest hit.

The nursery school building programme resulting from plans to expand nursery education made when Margaret Thatcher was Secretary of State for Education has been cut. In many areas new nurseries which have been built stand empty. Authorities say that they cannot afford to equip or staff them.

College courses are cut at the very time when the decline in industry is reducing the number of apprenticeships available, and yet a shortage of skilled, trained man and woman power is holding back this country's economic growth.

Some local authorities are asking permission to save money by lowering the standard of school meals, but a London University nutrition survey found that many children are already getting less than the minimum standards laid down for school meals. 5% of the children in the survey had nothing else to eat each day but cereal and bread and jam. The need for a nutritious midday meal at school grows as unemployment affects more families.

Already school milk has been abolished for children over eleven and in some areas for the seven to elevens. There have been cuts in the provision of cheap milk and welfare foods for expectant mothers and the under-fives.

The cuts in the Health Service are the most savage of all. There has been a complete standstill in overall Health Service spending, and yet reorganisation has resulted in the employment of many more highly paid administrators, so the cuts are made where they hurt the patients most — in the wards, outpatient and casualty departments.

Local papers throughout the country carry stories of hospitals closing, while plans for new buildings which would have replaced them are scrapped. Accident and emergency services in many hospitals are being cut back from round the clock to 9—5 openings, or being closed completely.

It is working class areas that are hardest hit. Sheffield, the centre of the steel industry, has no major burns unit.

In East London and in Liverpool, the hospitals nearest the docks have been closed. Ambulances carrying dockworkers speed past the darkened hospitals and tangle with traffic on congested roads to reach an open hospital several miles further on.

Hospital closures put an extra strain on ambulance services since patients must travel further, and many who could have walked to a hospital near

Bootle and Stanley Hospital near Liverpool docks — closed

their home must now call out an ambulance, yet in the name of economy ambulance services too have been cut.

It is commonplace for patients with eleven o'clock outpatient appointments to be collected from their homes at eight in the morning and left sitting after their treatment until four or five in the afternoon, waiting to be taken home. They dare not leave the draughty corridors in which they wait in search of a bite to eat or a cup of tea in case the ambulance comes for them. Drivers have to fit in picking up elderly, infirm and disabled patients between emergency calls. Once the two services were separate.

Waiting lists for treatment grow, and some patients die because the treatment is not available. There are children with kidney trouble whose lives could be saved, but the two specialized units in London where they could be given dialysis while waiting for transplants are not being given the money they need to take in new patients. Each unit needs £150,000 to keep going for another year, yet every year £38m of NHS money is given to drug companies to pay the cost of advertising in medical journals.

In East London, where infant mortality is higher than in other parts of the country, doctors are convinced that the lack of proper facilities in two of the maternity hospitals is causing babies to die unnecessarily.

Maternity services have improved enormously since the pre-war days when most babies were delivered without medical help and often by unqualified midwives. Then many babies died. Now there are plans to cut these services, and doctors believe that babies' lives will be put at risk once more. Maternity services need to be improved, not cut.

In order to cut costs, some hospitals are sacking their own trainee nurses when they pass their exams and become qualified. It is cheaper to cut down on qualified, experienced staff and rely on students.

An engineering worker from North Wales whose wife is a nurse told how they had both applied for jobs all over the country with no success. In one hospital after another she had been told,

> *"We would love to offer you a job, we need more staff,*
> *but we haven't enough money to employ all our own*
> *students when they qualify."*

Another economy is achieved by cutting the average time that patients stay in hospital. It has fallen from three weeks to ten days since the Health Service started. Part of the drop has resulted from better anaesthetics, new drugs and treatment, but often patients are sent home before they feel really well, and it is expected that the family and the district nurse will cope.

Uncleaned windows, surgical ward

There is a great deal of propaganda for community care. People should be taken from institutions to be cared for in the more natural setting of the community, we are told. So patients are sent home from mental hospitals or found rooms in boarding houses; elderly people who would once have stayed on in hospital are sent home too. This places an enormous burden on families, usually on the women, because the facilities which would make community care a reality are simply not there. Local authority health services — home helps, modifications to old or disabled people's homes, free telephones, day centres for the mentally handicapped or disabled, old people's homes or communal flats, hostels for discharged mental patients — these services were never adequate, but what little provision there was is being slashed.

Where there is no family to take the burden, old people live alone, confined to bed or chair, waiting for the district nurse to help them dress. A home help may come for an hour or so to clean and shop, and the meals on wheels service, if it has not been cut, will bring food at mid-day.

Similar arguments are being used to persuade mothers that small children are better off at home or with child-minders than in a day nursery or nursery school where they could be cared for by trained staff. Yet a survey in South London found that more than 40% of women who were on their own all day with under-fives suffered from clinical depression. That means not just that they were fed up and isolated, but that they were depressed to the point of needing medical treatment.

The strain of coping with children and the struggle to manage on a single wage when nurseries are not available to provide care for children while mothers go out to work turns every high-rise block into a giant box of tranquillizers.

Of course it is far cheaper for local authorities to rely on child-minders than to provide nurseries. Only eight nursery places for every thousand children under five are planned for 1983, although a hundred and thirty-seven mothers out of every thousand with children under five go out to work for at least 18 hours a week. There are 100,000 children cared for by child-minders and most of their mothers would prefer them to be in nurseries. Some children who have been passed from minder to minder start school without having learned to play. Some cannot even talk.

While some authorities cut major sections of expenditure altogether, sacking large numbers of workers, others try to soften the blow and achieve economies by piecemeal and often petty measures. They limit redundancy to 'natural wastage' — not replacing people who leave. This reduces union opposition, but still cuts the total number of jobs available. Some Councils transfer to contractors work which was once done by the local authority employees. In some areas it is the dustmen who have been replaced by contract workers, in others delivery drivers. The change relieves the Council of the obligation to pay union rates and keep to union agreements controlling working conditions.

Another petty economy tried by some hospitals and education authorities has been not to renew the work permits of immigrant workers, securing redundancies in this way. In one London borough, prompt action by a school union representative and the local union branch saved over a dozen teachers from losing their work permits. Some unions have been less prompt to act, and their officials have been prepared to listen to arguments that the jobs of English workers should be protected before those of members from abroad, as if there were first and second-class union members. Workers whose permits are not renewed lose not only their jobs but the life they have built in this country, because they face deportation. In its effects this economy is racialist.

Apart from cuts in major services, health, transport, education and welfare services, there is a general decline in amenities which results from cuts in local authority expenditure. Roads are left dirty, parks and gardens neglected, dustbins are emptied less often, libraries cut their opening hours and have fewer books to lend.

The unemployed, with time on their hands, find that every facility which could have helped them make better use of that time is in decline or gone. Using the public library, taking up evening classes, going for a swim or taking the kids to the park — all these opportunities are dwindling because of the cuts.

Only one Council has had the guts to take a stand and refuse to cut the services it knows that people need — the Council of a small Derbyshire mining village, Clay Cross. In 1973 they refused to raise Council rents and cut council services and council workers' wages when instructed to do so by the Tory government, and for that the councillors were barred from office and fined. The Labour Party in opposition pledged support for them and their stand, but once in office the Labour government refused to fulfil their pledge and embarked on new cuts.

Each change in the economic situation brings a new excuse to justify further cuts. When the slump was at its worst, workers were told that public expenditure must be cut and funds released to industry to finance investment. These funds could not come from the profits of the rich; they must come from the services provided for the working people. The trade union movement accepted these arguments, and agreed to sacrifice the education of their children, the welfare of the old, the needs of the homeless.

Then the recovery began, and in July 1976 more cuts were announced. This time the Chancellor, Denis Healey, claimed it was essential to cut public expenditure because the recovery was going a little faster than had been expected. We needed to borrow money from abroad to finance the expansion, and to gain the bankers' confidence we must demonstrate our willingness to make sacrifices. So expenditure must be cut by a further thousand million pounds. The cuts would mean the loss of at least seventy thousand jobs, amongst them civil servants, nurses, teachers and local authority workers. Backing up the Chancellor's call for these cuts, the Prime Minister brought out the blackmail, so effective with the trade union leaders — if the trade union movement did not accept the cuts, the government would fall and the Tories come back. Anyway, said Callaghan, "They will not be savage cuts — merely the removal of a little of the surplus." Cuts of £1,000,000,000 — the equivalent of the total budget of the National Health Service — "just a little of the surplus". The surplus lives of babies, the surplus opportunities of schoolchildren and the surplus care of the sick.

Every time that public expenditure cuts put public service workers onto the dole queue, every time that industrial unemployment rises, government income falls. Unemployed people pay no tax, and they have to be paid their dole and supplementary benefit out of public funds. So each new round of cuts which causes unemployment reduces further still the money available for public services and leads to yet another round of cuts.

One and a half million people on the dole costs at least fifteen million pounds in taxes lost *every week* and at least thirty million pounds paid out in benefits — well over £2,000m a year. The vicious circle of cuts is inescapable if the government is determined to play the game according to the capitalists' rules.

The Labour government, pledged to ideas of welfare and equality, is steadily following policies which will bring us nearer and nearer to the Tory ideal of a Free Enterprise Britain. The social services are being cut to the bone, and those in need are more and more exposed to the cruel chaos of capitalism.

5. WHERE THE AXE FALLS— WHO GOES FIRST

As unemployment increases, whether as a result of cuts in public spending or closures and redundancies in industry, the first workers to be sent down the road are those who are most vulnerable — women, young workers and school leavers, the disabled, older workers, immigrants and black workers.

Job Centre

Women workers are among the first to go. Cuts in public spending throw home helps, cleaners, hospital manual workers, nurses and teachers onto the dole. The vast majority of these are women.

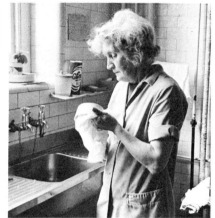
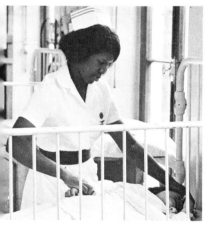

When shops close down, or cut down on staff because people no longer have money to spend, more women are out of work.

As demand falls, especially in industries like food manufacture, many firms cut out their part-time shifts, staffed almost entirely by women. Because part-timers are hard to organise into unions, the unions may not be prepared to put up a fight when their jobs are threatened. Even union leaders swallow the fallacy that women work for frills and luxuries.

At Smiths Industries, an engineering factory in Cricklewood, North West London, nineteen women were sacked from the twilight shift without a murmur from the union. In an infamous case in the Post Office in Birmingham the union actually organized the sacrifice of the jobs of 72 part-time women workers, who had been there for up to twenty years, to preserve the overtime of their male members.

The sacked women were union members too, and one of them said,

> *"During the post-office workers' strike in 1972, the girls manned the picket line, those part-timers, the same ones that have left. It was the girls who were there day after day in the cold, because it was winter. And very hard up, believe me. We used to share what coppers we had to give to those who needed it for bus fares home. It was very difficult for seven weeks."*

Between January and June 1975, unemployment among women rose by 121%. Among men in the same period it rose by 48%. This figure reflects only the rise among those registering as unemployed. Many women do not bother to register because they pay reduced national insurance contributions and do not qualify for unemployment benefit.

A survey published in WOMAN'S OWN in March, 1976, found that of women seeking work, only three in ten were registered as unemployed.

The true total of jobless in that month was well over two million. Many women who need or want to go out to work cannot make suitable arrangements for the care of their children, especially now nurseries and playcentres are being cut.

Social service cuts also force women back into the home to care for elderly or disabled relatives.

Some people argue that women have only themselves to blame when they are the first to suffer from unemployment and the cuts. They are accused of not being prepared to play their part in union organization, of not being prepared to fight. The story of the Birmingham Post Office workers illustrates some of the problems women meet within the union. Pressures of home and family certainly make it harder for women to organize than it is for men. Militant trade unionists should campaign for union meetings in work time or the provision of creches to overcome some of these problems, and recognize that the sharing of work in the home between men and women is essential if women are to play their full part in union affairs. Certainly when women do organize they are capable of fighting every bit as fiercely as men.

The women who had been striking for equal pay at Trico Folberth in West London for thirteen weeks had to face convoys of lorries with concealed number plates which burst through their picket lines in the early hours of the morning escorted by coachloads of police. This only strengthened their determination to fight on.

This was six months after 'Equal Pay Day' — New Year's Day 1976 when equal pay supposedly became law.

The 4½% deal abandoned all progress towards 'equal pay', but even when the £6 limit was in force and progress towards equal pay supposedly allowed, women workers soon learned that it was only achieved if they were prepared to fight for it.

Women can organize against redundancies.

When Carol went to work in a Liverpool printing factory, part of a large combine, she found that although the women were all union members, they were not involved in the work of the union. There was only one woman on the shop stewards' committee to represent all their interests, even though women were in a majority in the factory.

She decided to change this situation. There were a few women in each department prepared to cooperate with her, and together they worked patiently for a year to build up the women workers' confidence.

They produced bulletins about conditions in the factory and outside problems such as inflation and unemployment. They discussed the day-to-day problems of the shopfloor, and the issues raised in the Union Journal. During this year, Carol and some of the others were elected onto the shop stewards' committee, and the women workers had gained enough confidence to go into the office and take up grievances themselves, with their stewards' backing.

Soon after, management announced that the factory was in financial difficulties and there would have to be a hundred redundancies, mostly among the women, if the factory was not to close. The men on the shop stewards' committee were prepared to accept the redundancies. The women were not. They argued with their members that the management's bluff should be called.

They decided not to argue on the financial basis of the combine, although it was extremely profitable, since they thought the other workers would say, whatever the state of the combine as a whole, if this factory is financially disastrous and losing them money, they will close it. So Carol describes the arguments they used:

"What we said was, 'We are faced with a situation in Liverpool where unemployment is really high. Children are coming out of school; you're going to accept these hundred redundancies, you're going to sell these jobs out of the labour market for ever, because they will never, ever reappear inside Merseyside. It might be a hundred jobs here, but it's happening all over Merseyside. Now you must be responsible to keep these jobs and have them existing inside the labour market for your children coming out of school. It's your responsibility.' That had a tremendous effect."

A full factory meeting rejected the redundancies. A year of consistent hard work and principled argument had created a situation where, as Carol said:

"Women would stand up nose to nose with the union officials and say, 'We're telling you what WE want. You sit down and listen to us. You're asking us to accept redundancies. We're not going to accept.' The workforce said point blank that they would not accept any redundancies, and the management never ever came up with a policy of closing the plant or sacking those hundred people.

They did put up a notice saying that they would accept voluntary redundancies, and for a period we had a real hard battle to stop people going into Personnel and applying for voluntary redundancy. If they did apply for voluntary redundancy their union card would be taken away, and they would not get another job in the printing industry in Liverpool."

In arguing against the proposed redundancies, the women in this factory showed their concern for young people leaving school and seeking work. While unemployment nationally is between 5% and 6% of the insured population, for under 25s it is more than 11%.

Young people leave school to face an aimless life on the dole. Some continue their education hoping that more qualifications will improve their chances of finding a job, but the cuts are reducing even these opportunities. Either way students leaving school or college find that there are no jobs for them, and as firms close down or cut their labour force, the number of apprenticeships available drops as well.

A lecturer in a technical college in North West London said that he has arrived prepared to teach a class of apprentices on day release only to find the lecture room empty because firms had closed and the apprenticeships ceased.

The waste of talent, hope and idealism represented by youth unemployment is tragic.

An unemployed miner from Dunfermline, now 23, recalls how it felt to be unemployed when he was younger:

"Then, being on the dole was just an emptiness. A feeling of being outside everything, you know? Things happening, like society going on outside you. You did na' feel complete, did na' feel a real man. I didn't have any real dignity, and I got real hurt when people said to me, 'Oh, you're on the dole,' you know? And it made me feel workshy, things like this. And then immediately you get a job people's attitude changes towards you, and immediately you're a responsible member of society, but you know inside yourself that you're no different. You're just the same as you were on the dole."

The government's response to union pressure to provide more jobs for school leavers has been the Job Creation Programme. Schemes put forward by local authorities or charitable bodies are granted money. Some of the schemes are imaginative and provide opportunities for those taking part to learn new skills, but most consist of labouring work like scrubbing graffiti off walls, clearing overgrown cemeteries or cleaning beaches, and seem to be designed simply to keep the teenagers off the streets. Some have an Alice-through-the-Looking-Glass quality — there are young people on a job creation scheme making a house-to-house survey in one area to find out what facilities and services people need, while the cuts ensure that there will be no chance of these needs being met when they are revealed. After six or twelve months, when the schemes come to an end, the young workers are back on the dole queue.

After months without work and refusals of job after job, many young people turn to the army, the police and the other services rather than remain dependent on their families. In 1975—6, army recruitment rose by 24%. For these recruits the most likely prospect is facing bombs and bullets in the streets of Belfast. The situation in Northern Ireland and the reluctance to face service there led to a drop in recruitment in the early seventies, but unemployment has increased it once more.

When young people can find work, it is often so badly paid that they get very little more than they would have done from social security. They also find that many employers regard them as a source of cheap temporary labour, to be sacked on the flimsiest of pretexts before they have worked long enough to be entitled to protection either from the union or from legislation.

Kerry is 16. She comes from Fazackerley near Liverpool, and says: "When I left school last year, there were hundreds of us looking for work." Not all of them found jobs, and since then 4,000 more school leavers have joined the queues in Liverpool.

For Kerry herself there followed a succession of poorly paid, short-lived jobs punctuated by periods of unemployment. One was in the sewing machine shop in a factory. Pay was 45p an hour. Kerry wanted to join the union in the factory — USDAW, the shop workers' union.

> "They said I'd to do four weeks before they allowed me to join the union. I asked them about it, asked the union rep and he said after my four weeks were up I could join the union. I was sacked as soon as my four weeks were finished. I went to the union rep, asked if he could do anything for me. He said no, I wasn't in the union, so that was that one gone."

Her next job was as a premium caller in a Bingo hall.

> "The conditions were terrible. There was no union there. I was trying to talk to the girls about unions. That was after about two weeks — I was sacked."

Four months of unemployment followed, then a job at 32½p an hour as a sewing machinist in a family firm near the Liverpool town centre. The firm was strongly anti-union, and although the workers were nominally unionized in the Tailors and Garment Workers Union, they were not organized. When Kerry asked the union representative in the factory about joining, she was told to wait until the district rep called. He came, and asked Kerry detailed questions about how she had got on at school and whether she could get a reference from her school to enable her to join the union.

Local trade union officials often complain that young people show little interest in unions, and it is hard to get them to join.

Like the young, older workers bear more than their fair share of the burden of unemployment, finding increasingly that it is impossible to get another job when they are made redundant. Even skilled men with twenty or thirty years of service in a single firm, who think that their experience will be welcomed, find that they are considered too old to start again, or simply that there are no jobs.

Some of them have been persuaded to take voluntary redundancy. The lump sum is a considerable temptation. They decide not to fight the closure of the factory or the contraction of the labour force. After all, there is a lump sum, more money than most working people ever handle in a lifetime, and six months on earnings related unemployment benefit, which should allow time to find a new job.

The reality is often different. The lump sum soon goes. After six months earnings-related benefit comes to an end and there may be anything up to five years on supplementary benefit before the time comes to draw a pension. In this situation the redundancy scheme that seemed so attractive becomes like the pot of gold at the end of the rainbow that turns to dust when you grasp it.

Disabled workers too, whose contribution is welcomed by employers at times of full employment, find work very hard to get when unemployment rises. Employers, free to pick and choose, give preference to the fittest applicants for jobs.

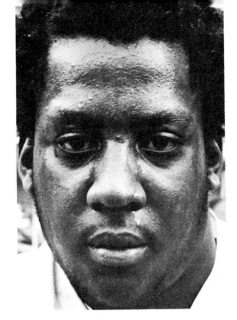

Young people are among the hardest hit by unemployment, but to be young and black is to face rebuff after rebuff in the search for work.

Leroy left school with five 'O' levels. He went for an interview for a post which had required three or more 'O' levels, taking his certificate with him. He was told,

> "You know something, you're a well-built kid, you've got
> a lot of strength in you. Why don't you do a job like a
> labourer, you know, picking up heavy things. You earn
> good money. Or be a weightlifter?"

Leroy was surprised. He said he'd only come for a job and he'd got the five 'O' levels which were acceptable to them.

They said, "This ain't your sort of job, you look energetic. Do you play football? You don't want this sort of job, it's boring." The job went to the other applicant who had three 'O' levels, but was white.

After meeting a succession of such rejections, some young blacks decide that they don't care, feel that they have no future and give up the search for a job.

All immigrants are hard hit by unemployment. Many work in public sector jobs — hospital, transport, local authority services — which are being cut. Others work in small businesses, small component factories supplying the motor industry, for instance, which are being forced to close by the recession, or in declining industries like textiles. Whatever the industry, immigrant workers are often the first to lose their jobs as a result of 'first-in, last-out' agreements.

In the eighteen months to May 1975, while unemployment rose on average by 65%, the rise was 156% for West Indian, Asian and African Britons and 182% for young West Indians.

At the same time discrimination in the whole society increases. The insecurity caused by high unemployment makes people more ready to listen to racialist propaganda.

At present the National Front and the National Party campaign more openly and with some success, preying on people's fears of losing their jobs. The press, far from contradicting their propaganda, encourage them by indulging in hysterical campaigns like the one against the Asian refugees from Malawi who were temporarily housed by the council in a four-star hotel at Gatwick.

For politicians, it is quite convenient if people blame immigrants for unemployment and falling living standards instead of blaming them, so Members of Parliament and councillors from both Parties make speeches about 'invasion' and say, 'Enough is enough' — Bob Mellish, Labour M.P., 'Brent cannot take any more' — Alderman Hartley, leader of Brent's Labour Council. These speeches reach the headlines and serve to make racialism respectable, while Enoch Powell's speeches incite racialists to violence.

In June 1976 Powell spoke in Parliament, prophesying racial violence. Such prophecies are self-fulfilling — within a fortnight three black youths and one white had been murdered solely because of their race.

In Blackburn there were violent scenes when a councillor from the National Party attacked a Labour councillor. Later he discharged himself from hospital rather than be treated by a black doctor.

For many years, when there was full employment, immigrants arrived in this country in far greater numbers than they do now. When jobs were plentiful, people came; when there were few jobs, immigration dropped. Now, although immigration controls are so stringent that it can take up to three years for dependents to get permission to join members of their families in Britain, people are given the false impression that millions of immigrants are pouring in.

In the nineteen thirties, when there were hardly any black people living in this country, unemployment was higher, housing conditions were worse, and the standard of living of working people lower than it is today.

At that time Hitler in Germany and Mosley and his blackshirts in Britain tried to convince people that the Jews were the cause of their problems. Mosley was driven from the East End by the united resistance of Jewish and English workers.

Many of the leaders of the National Front and the National Party were supporters of Hitler and Mosley at that time. Some still go to Germany regularly to celebrate Hitler's birthday and meet with fascists from other countries. They can be defeated by united resistance from black and white workers who are prepared to stand up against their racist lies and their violence, and this resistance is being organized within the immigrant communities and among all those opposed to racism.

73

6. LIVING ON THE DOLE

'Eat more fruit!' the slogans say,
*   'More fish, more beef, more bread!'*
But I'm on unemployment pay
*   My third year now, and wed.*

And so I wonder when I'll see
*   The slogan when I pass,*
The only one that would suit me, —
*   'Eat more bloody grass!'*

Joe Corrie.

Jarrow 1936

Remembering the thirties when she helped organize the Jarrow March, Mrs. Clark said:

> "I don't think things could ever be so bad again. You see what we didn't have then we have now, the most wonderful welfare state that ever was. I think everybody agrees with that. You've got all the assistance in the world. No one goes hungry these days."

Jarrow 1976

Mary too comes from Tyneside. Jobs there are still scarce, especially for those who are neither perfectly fit nor skilled. Her husband has been out of work since he injured his back in an accident at work six years ago.

"The children can't understand why they never have a holiday. They can't understand why they don't get new clothes like their friends do. We try to tell them, but they can't understand. It's a strain when they cry, you know, they really cry. At Christmas they won't go out of the house because the others are bragging about what they've got."

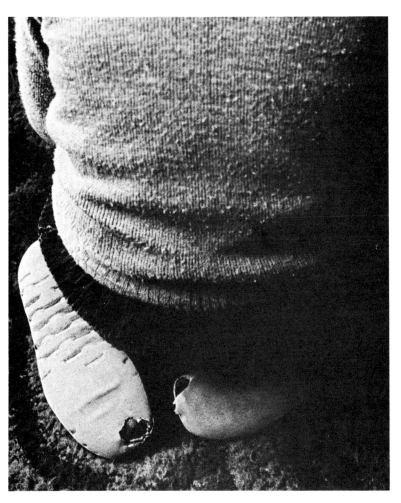

A survey published by the Child Poverty Action Group found that families living at supplementary benefit level rely on filling food — baked beans, bread and margarine, potatoes and sugar — at the expense of health. They cannot afford more than half the average amount spent by other families on meat, bacon and fish. Even eggs and milk have to be cut down.

Mary finds that the children are always ailing, and always seem to be hungry. And Gary is fussy — "He won't eat half the things I can afford to give him."

Getting food for the family is worry enough, but children perpetually need new shoes, and then the bills come in:

"There's such a song and dance about bills — £30 for the gas, £11 just for the lights. I can't pay the bills so I just put them up above the mantelpiece and look at them."

Marcus, still young, prepared to move to any part of the country where he can find both a job and a home for his family, says:

"The worst thing, the thing that really gets you down, is the uncertainty: that you've got no future. The future is the next electricity bill and whether you can pay that."

He recently finished a government retraining scheme to become a carpenter, but nobody wants to take him on when there are skilled and experienced carpenters down at the dole. He has the skill and the time to improve his home, but:

"If you want to put up some shelves, even if you've got the wood left over from something else, you find you can't afford to go out and buy the brackets. I could have repainted the whole damn house, but I can't afford to go out and buy paint."

Unemployment isolates families and destroys their social life. Friends from work lose touch, people cannot afford to go out, and are often ashamed to invite people into their homes because they have become shabby and worn.

The Department of Health and Social Security is permitted to give grants to meet special needs, but not permitted to tell people about them, and in any case the cuts have made them more grudging than ever. An unemployed welfare rights worker said:

"I've noticed of late that these discretionary payments for clothing, electricity bills, etc., are just not being paid at all now, as far as I can see. You used to be able to go in there and argue for them and win them, but now they just pay you your flat rate and if you go under, well you can sink as far as they're concerned."

Every penny has to be justified to the DHSS officials, and they have enormous powers to limit or refuse benefits.

Joe left his wife and five children in Salford and took a job in Lincoln with the promise of a house for all the family as soon as one was vacant. For four and a half months he worked for wages which were lower than the money he would have been getting on the dole. He had to pay for his lodgings and send money home to support his family. All his spare time was spent tramping round looking for a new home for all of them.

At last he went to the manager of the Lincoln Employment Exchange and explained the position to him. The manager advised him to return to Salford. There was little chance of a council house, he said, and even less of finding a privately rented one. He assured Joe that he could not be penalized for leaving his job after the efforts he had made.

Joe returned to Salford and went to sign on. He describes the reception he got.

> *"The clerk said, 'Well, if you left the job of your own accord, your dole's stopped for six weeks.'*
>
> *I said, 'Will you please phone the manager of the exchange in Lincoln. He knows all the circumstances.'*
>
> *'We're not interested in that. We contact your last employer, not the office in Lincoln.'*
>
> *'Surely to God,' I said, 'there's no harm for you to get in touch with your department in another town sooner than penalize me for something I had no control over.'*
>
> *'After six weeks we'll start making inquiries.'*
>
> *'I'm not taking punishment for six weeks and then finding myself innocent. I thought in this country you were innocent until proven guilty, but you want me to actually serve my sentence and then prove my innocence. Not on my life, I won't.' "*

Joe insisted and was given his full benefit. Anyone less persistent could have faced six weeks without benefit.

This kind of treatment from officials and continual refusals when they seek work make many people feel personally responsible for being unemployed.

Forty years ago George Orwell wrote, in THE ROAD TO WIGAN PIER,

> "When I first saw unemployed men at close quarters, the thing that horrified me was to find that many of them were ashamed of being unemployed . . . I remember the shock of astonishment it gave me . . . to find that a fair proportion of these beings whom I had been taught to regard as cynical parasites were decent young miners and cotton workers . . . They had been brought up to work, and it seemed as if they were never going to have the chance of working again. In their circumstances it was inevitable, at first, that they should be haunted by a feeling of personal degradation. That was the attitude towards unemployment in those days: it was a disaster which happened to you as an individual and for which you were to blame."

In 1976 a young unemployed engineering worker describes the same feeling:

> "I was very down because I'd written what, 150, 200 letters for jobs, drawing only one interview that I didn't get the job for. On average there's anything between three and four hundred people going for a job. I mean one does become very demoralized.
>
> I saw a lass I knew coming to sign on. She's usually a nice, lively, cheerful sort of lass. She's always smiling, always nice to you. As she came down, she had her coat collar turned up, and dark glasses on, and she was huddled down, and she was so depressed. You know, it was like the end of the world. I mean she'd only been out a couple of months, but you get to that point very quickly.
>
> A lot of people who don't understand why there's unemployment at this time in such large numbers get the idea that they themselves personally are failing, that they're just not good enough, that's why they don't get a job. That's just not true in this situation."

Working class Londoners, 1863

This attitude is not accidental, it is part of the whole Poor Law tradition which reached its zenith in Victorian times. The employers of the industrial revolution needed a flexible labour force for their mills and factories. They took on more workers or laid them off to suit the fluctuations of trade. Farmers did the same, hiring more labour at harvest and other busy times. When their labour was not needed, workers were thrown onto parish relief.

True to the contradictions of Victorian morality, while employers felt no responsibility to keep workers on or maintain them through slack times, they held that the unemployed did not work because they lacked the virtues of industry, frugality and prudence. In 1834 the Poor Law Act was amended to end the practice of paying 'outdoor relief' to people in their homes. All those seeking relief were forced into the workhouse. Many new workhouses were built and were nicknamed Bastilles. One assistant Poor Law Commissioner wrote, "Our intention is to make the workhouses as much like prisons as possible." Another made clear the intention: "To establish therein a discipline so severe and repulsive as to make them a terror to the poor and prevent them from entering."

Paupers were stripped of all their possessions. Men were separated from women, and children over three taken from their mothers. All were set to hard and often useless task work.

Those who managed to survive outside the workhouse were visited by Ladies Bountiful — probably the wives and daughters of the very employers who had caused their destitution. They dispensed broth, tracts and cast-off clothing to those they considered deserving of their generosity.

82

These Victorian attitudes survived into the thirties in the means test, which denied benefit to the unemployed if there was any other source of household income. Many people can remember trinkets and furniture being passed over back walls in working class streets as the 'means test' men came to the front doors. One man recalls that he and his mother were refused benefit because they had three chairs for a household of two.

Reminiscences and novels of those years have many descriptions of the operation of these measures. One of the best of these is Walter Greenwood's LOVE ON THE DOLE. It is set in a Salford where the only people in work were the assistants at the pawn shops and the clerks at the Labour Exchange. He describes the scenes at the exchange on the day that the means test was introduced. One after another, the men are refused benefit because they have sons or daughters bringing in a pound or two a week. They are told that there is no appeal.

> *Outside the exchange, "A quite different atmosphere from usual enlivened the adjacent streets. Police were conspicuous. Knots of men barred pavements and roadways listening and interjecting as various spokesmen voiced heated criticisms of this, the latest economy of the National Government. Occasionally, the spokesmen's words would be lost in rowdy, jumbled torrents of cursings and abusive oaths. From the Labour exchange came a continuous trickle of men wearing appropriate expressions as became their individual dispositions. Men of Harry's kind dazed, mystified, staring at the ground; more spirited individuals flushed with anger, lips trembling with resentment."*

The unemployed marched to the Town Hall, to be met by police batons, and the book's hero dies in hospital from injuries received on the demonstration. Such scenes took place all over the country as resistance to the means test was organized by the National Unemployed Workers' Movement.

Overleaf — Searching for jobs in the 1930s

Another regulation under which the unemployed could be refused benefit was the 'not genuinely seeking work' clause.

Bill, a retired Post Office worker, now living in N.W. London, joined the army at seventeen, having been unable to find work, and was sent to Northern Ireland where he met and married an Irish girl. He realised that he was opposed to the army's role in Ireland and was able to leave on compassionate grounds. There was no work for him in Derry, so he and his wife struggled to live on her ten shillings a week wage as a maid. They appealed for help to the St. Vincent de Paul Society and were given a ticket which he said "could be exchanged for flour, tea, sugar and candles (no coal) evidently it was assumed that the flour could be baked into bread from the heat of the lighted candles."

Later he came to England, and found work, but not for long. Unemployed once more, he was called to appear before the Court of Referees which had to find out if he was genuinely seeking work. He says:

> *"Some jobs under the Employment Act were not insurable. These were gardeners, chauffeurs and others too numerous to mention. I was not aware of this at the time. When asked if I would take any job, I replied, 'Yes'. I was disallowed benefit on the grounds that I was not genuinely seeking insurable employment."*

He was referred to the Public Assistant Committee which administered the means test.

> *"I received visits from their investigators who searched my room for any luxurious items which might be hidden away and could be sold before any money was paid out. They looked everywhere for stocks of food which I might have been hoarding. They were ruthless individuals and almost always smelt of drink. I had then to appear before a committee who in no uncertain terms expressed the view that I was a parasite sponging on society.*
>
> *The committee chairman was the wife of Admiral Taylor, Tory MP for South Paddington. Also sitting at this half-round table was a clergyman who was so fat that his belly was resting on the table. There were about a dozen well-fed ladies and gentlemen who made up the committee."*

They offered Bill a ticket for the workhouses. He replied that they could make out the ticket for his wife and child but he would not be going there. He was asked to wait outside.

> *"A policeman was stationed at the door of the committee room. This was because some people lost their temper at the insulting remarks of the committee members when the interview was taking place and they sometimes kicked the table over."*

They kept him waiting for about an hour and then informed him that his benefit was to be extended for six weeks.

People claiming benefit are still treated as though they were spongers, skivers and malingerers, although, while the DHSS estimate that £4m was wrongfully claimed from them in 1975, the Inland Revenue believes that £500m was lost in tax evasion. Yet the Inland Revenue brought only 126 prosecutions compared with the 15,350 brought by the DHSS.

A report by the Political and Economic Planning Research group says that most of those who claim benefit but have no intention of working are well-to-do people who have retired early on company pensions. This is very different from the picture of 'scroungers' presented by the popular press.

The humiliations faced by the unemployed and their families and the continual strain of poverty can lead to despair. Mary said:

> *"I think I'll end up in the hospital, the asylum. I do. I many times think that I'm going there now. You see no end to it though. You don't see an end to it. You wish they were older, you hadn't got a husband who couldn't get a job . . ."*

For others the frustration leads to a determination to fight the system which has forced them into an unacceptable situation. For Marcus the greatest frustration is:

> *"The knowing, the feeling that you're bloody useless, that you can't contribute anything. Here you are with a family and at the time of your life when you want to be doing something constructive, building up a future for them, and there's nothing you can do. You're just forced to sit on your arse and take it or get off your arse and organize."*

Despite the temptation to give into despair, or to concentrate every energy on the business of making ends meet, the unemployed are fighting back.

Individuals appeal against the harsh rulings of the administrators, and many appeals are successful, especially when claimants take with them an experienced trade unionist, or a member of their local Right to Work Committee or Claimants' Union.

Collectively, the unemployed are organizing with the employed to resist the necessity for unemployment and achieve the right to work.

7. THE FIGHT BACK

As workers organize, the existence of a pool of unemployed threatens their every gain.

Engels wrote of the unemployed in 1878, in an article explaining Marx's CAPITAL:

> *"They form an industrial reserve army, which is paid* below *the value of its labour and is irregularly employed, or comes under the care of public Poor Law institutions during times of bad or moderate business, but which is indispensable to the capitalist class at times when business is especially lively, but which* under all circumstances *serves to break the power of resistance of the regularly employed workers and to keep their wages down."*

Mrs. Clark remembers what it was like to be one of the few who had work in Jarrow in the 1930s:

> *"I got into a job. In those days there were so many for one job you just made sure you weren't going to lose your job by doing or saying anything out of line. You really kept in step to keep your job because you knew you could so easily be out of work the next day because there was twenty, a couple of dozen for your job."*

A high level of unemployment makes it easier for employers to victimize militant workers, and harder to organize resistance against the victimization.

A fight among dockers waiting for work, 1949

In 1971, a year of comparative expansion, the working class movement was able to secure the release from Pentonville of the five jailed dockers, and they got their jobs back. But by the time twenty-four building workers were brought to trial for picketing against the Lump during the official building workers' strike of 1972 the trade union movement was unable to organize sufficient resistance to prevent three of them being sent to prison, or to get them out once they were there. In fact when Ricky Tomlinson, one of the jailed pickets who had recently been released, went to the 1975 Trades Union Congress asking to speak on behalf of Des Warren, who was still inside, Marie Paterson from the chair threatened to call the police to remove him. Since the trial, the twenty-four Shrewsbury building workers have had to contend with the blacklist which operates against them and other militants in the building industry.

One of them said:

> *"They told me at the exchange that they would have to tell the employers who I was. I said I didn't mind. They've got my picture up in every site office around here anyway."*

Militants have always recognized that if the divisive threat of unemployment is to be destroyed the unemployed must be organized alongside the employed workers.

The 1880s were years of strikes and agitation out of which were formed the general unions which today are the Transport Workers' and General and Municipal Workers' unions. Until then the trade unions had organized skilled workers only within their trades. These two new unions were the first to organize the unskilled across the boundaries of craft and industry.

Among the struggles of the '80s were two famous East End strikes — the strike of the matchgirls at Bryant and May in Poplar, and the strike for the Dockers' Tanner. One of the leaders of the dock strike was Tom Mann, who three years earlier had been one of the organizers of demonstrations by the unemployed.

Demonstrations of unemployed — 1878

Dockers' strike meeting, 1889

1886 was a year of slump and high unemployment. A march was organized to coincide with the Lord Mayor's Show. Banned from the route of the procession, the unemployed marched instead to Trafalgar Square and broke through a double police cordon to hold a meeting of thousands.

The City, frightened by the strength of the movement, set up a Lord Mayor's fund from which councils could draw to provide relief or work for the unemployed. Money poured in.

Trafalgar Square, 1886

Tom Mann was also a leader of the campaign for the eight-hour day, realizing that the call for a shorter working week was one which united employed and unemployed workers, because if achieved it would provide more jobs.

At that time unemployed workers who were union members drew some benefit from their union. The rest were forced to rely on begging, charity handouts or parish relief.

In the last years of the nineteenth century unemployed workers were organized to march through the better-off areas of London collecting money which was then divided up among those taking part in the march. These marches kept the problems of the unemployed in the public eye, and pricked the conscience of the well to do. But they fitted too neatly into a society which accepted unemployment as a personal misfortune to be alleviated by charitable bounty, and so undermined demands that unemployment should be eliminated by the provision of work or the payment of maintenance.

March of unemployed, London, 1903

These demands were pressed for by a national Right to Work movement which grew up in the early years of this century. Right to Work committees were set up all over the country between 1904 and 1908. In 1905 there were riots in Manchester and in 1907 a march was organized to the Victoria Embankment by contingents from every quarter of outer London.

March of the Right to Work Campaign, London 1908

With the election of the first Labour members to the House of Commons and slight improvements in the economic situation the emphasis of the campaign for the unemployed shifted towards Parliament and the call for a national system of insurance which would provide a guaranteed minimum income for those who were out of work. This was introduced in 1910 as part of Lloyd George's National Insurance scheme.

After the first World War Lloyd George's election campaign promised a land fit for heroes. Instead, thousands of ex-servicemen found themselves returning from the trenches to join the dole queue. There were never less than a million out of work in the inter-war years.

Unemployed ex-servicemen, Downing St, 1920

Unemployed women, January 1919

After the very short post-war boom a number of experienced militants among the unemployed began to organize.

One of these was Wal Hannington, and in his book, UNEMPLOYED STRUGGLES, he tells the story of the National Unemployed Workers' Movement.

The unemployed militants joined the existing organizations of the unemployed. They did not plan a concerted entry, but saw organizing among the unemployed as a natural extension of their experience of organizing in industry.

This experience made them aware of the need to stop the unemployed organizations being solely charity-seeking bodies, as they often were when the majority of the members were ex-servicemen. The militants understood the necessity of convincing the unemployed that they should not allow themselves to be used as blacklegs, and of convincing the official trade union movement of the need to encourage and cooperate with the organized unemployed.

During the engineers' national lockout in 1921 many members of the National Unemployed Workers' Movement were arrested. Some were released from prison after massive demonstrations outside the gates.

Unemployed march through the City, 1921

The first task of the National Unemployed Workers' Movement was to build an organization which would cover the whole country. They united many of the existing organizations of the unemployed on a district and then a national basis and recruited new members from the dole queues. Members paid a subscription of 1d a week. Branches provided help for members appealing against the petty bureaucrats administering the system of relief, and held meetings to which leaders of the movement were invited as speakers.

Some branches had premises where the unemployed could gather during the day. These premises had been provided sometimes by local councils in response to requests from the NUWM; in other areas branches occupied council premises which were standing idle. Many councils allowed them to keep the occupied premises or offered alternatives, but when a library was occupied in Islington the Islington council first cut off the water and electricity and then called on the police to evict the unemployed. The members barricaded themselves inside and held the premises, guarding them night and day for several weeks. Eventually, their vigilance slackened and 100 police raided the library at 5.30 one morning, turning the members out.

Unemployed workers from all over London marched on Islington Town Hall, intending to occupy it as a substitute for the lost library, but their plans must have leaked out, for the demonstrators were met by a large force of police whose batons fell mercilessly on demonstrators and bystanders, men, women and children alike.

Branches in the London area organized many raids on factories, such as the aircraft factory in Kilburn, where overtime was being worked.

The Glasgow branch was involved in constant battles against the eviction of unemployed workers from their homes for rent arrears. Together with the tenants' associations they built up a highly efficient warning system with scouts who ran or cycled through the streets to call out crowds of people to the scene of the eviction.

Harry McShane, the secretary of the Scottish NUWM, and a number of others moved an evicted tenant's furniture back into his house and barricaded themselves in. They sent away the bailiffs, asking them not to disturb the draughts tournament that was in progress. Meetings were held every two hours, with those in the house speaking to crowds in the street below. Food was hauled up on a rope. The police rushed the house late in the afternoon, arresting McShane and several others. But the campaign against evictions resulted in the Glasgow Council setting up a fund to help those who could not pay their rent.

The activities of the branches built up the national strength of the movement, and on Armistice Day 1922, less than a week before the arrival in London of the first national hunger marchers, twenty-five thousand unemployed ex-servicemen joined on the end of the official parade.

They marched with their medals pinned to their banners and pawn tickets on their coats, carrying a wreath with the inscription "From the living victims — the unemployed — to our dead comrades who died in vain". As the last contingent reached the Cenotaph, their band played the Red Flag and the International.

Hunger marchers in Hyde Park, 1923

On November 17th, more than two thousand unemployed who, with very little preparation, had spent up to a month on the road in bitter weather reached the capital. They had come from every part of the country, and their arrival was timed to coincide with the State Opening of Parliament on November 20th. Two days later they gathered in Whitehall. The newspapers, which had kept silent about the marchers for almost the whole time that they were on the road, now carried stories of impending riots and police preparations which included, according to one paper, the placing of machine guns on some of the buildings in Whitehall.

With the Russian Revolution fresh in their memory, the ruling class were apprehensive at the sight of vast crowds of unemployed demanding justice.

In spite of this apprehension, the Prime Minister, Bonar Law, refused to see a deputation of the marchers, so they decided to stay until he changed his mind. They held massive meetings and on one occasion congregated in the lobby of the House of Commons and called out a number of MPs before producing placards and drowning the debate in the chamber by singing the Red Flag.

The marchers stayed in the workhouses of the various London boroughs. When some had to return home for family reasons, contingents were sent to recruit reinforcements. The Ministry of Health, disturbed by this, ordered that these reinforcements should be treated as 'casuals' with a diet of bread and tea when they applied to the authorities for food and lodging on their routes. This led to conflict at every stopping place. One night at Luton marchers went out in twos or threes to cafes and restaurants in the town, ordered poached eggs and asked that the bill be sent to the Poor Law Guardians. In Rugby the marchers called a meeting in the town to keep the police busy while a few, including Hannington, went to the workhouse, took the store room keys from the terrified master and helped themselves to twenty-eight pots of jam. In the morning twenty-six marchers with empty jam pots held high on their stout walking sticks (two pots had broken) led the marchers to the workhouse. The jampot bearers fell out and deposited their empty pots in a neat pyramid on the workhouse steps in front of the master and his staff. Hannington was arrested once more a few days later and charged with feloniously stealing twenty-eight pots of jam! He was released when his fine was paid for him by a Quaker member of the Board of Guardians.

More great national hunger marches followed, one in 1929 against the 'not genuinely seeking work' clause of the National Insurance regulations under which many unemployed people were being struck off the register and denied support for themselves and their families.

This march received widespread support from working class people along the way, and the organizers believed that the publicity it gave to the plight of the unemployed and the government's failure to do anything about it contributed to the return of the Labour Government later that year.

Unfortunately the change of government did nothing to reduce unemployment and little to improve the conditions of the unemployed. The government was pledged to a policy of 'continuity'. Hannington describes it thus:

> *"One might say that the characteristic of the 1929 Labour Government was that of proving that capitalism was quite safe in the hands of the Labour administration."*

Labour politicians and the leaders of the TUC had given full support to the movement of the unemployed in the early years of the twenties, but, following the sell-out of the General Strike in 1926 and the rightward move of the trade union leaders in the period of working class defeat which followed, the TUC dissociated itself from the NUWM. When unemployed miners marched from the Welsh valleys to London in 1927, the TUC General Secretary, Walter Citrine, circulated all the Trades Councils on the route advising them not to render assistance to the marchers. The Trades Councils ignored these instructions and, with hundreds of rank-and-file workers and their families, provided a welcome, food, shelter and financial support for the marchers in every town they passed through. When the miners reached London, the Prime Minister refused to see them. Using the reactionary behaviour of the trade union leadership as a justification, he said he could not meet them because they did not have official backing.

The following year the Trades Union Congress, meeting in Swansea, refused to receive a deputation of unemployed miners while they listened eagerly to an address from the High Sheriff of Glamorgan.

Ramsay Macdonald dissolved his Labour Government in 1931 and formed the National Government which went to the country promising improvements in the unemployment situation under the combined leadership of the best brains of every party. In fact, the National Government was a Tory government with an ex-Labour Prime Minister.

Soon after the election, the unemployment figures reached three million — a record for that period — and the government reacted by cutting every public service, reducing wages and dole payments and introducing the infamous means test.

There were demonstrations against the means test and bloody battles outside employment exchanges in every part of the country. Police treatment of the unemployed was harsher than at any previous time, echoing the harsh measures of the government. And then, in the winter of 1931–2, another massive national hunger march — the two thousand five hundred marchers, including a special women's contingent, were met in Hyde Park by a hundred thousand London workers, employed and unemployed. They were also met by police baton charges. The forces of the police included large numbers of special constables who were especially hated because of the prominent role they had played during the General Strike. There was widespread fighting between police and unemployed around Marble Arch and Hyde Park Corner. Earlier, marchers had been attacked in the Edgware Road by mounted and foot police.

A contingent of hunger marchers nearing London, 1932

Tom Mann with the women's contingent of the Hunger March of 1932

Two days later a demonstration in the Whitehall area, waiting for the marchers' petition against the means test to be presented to Parliament, was again attacked by police.

1932 was a year of the highest unemployment in this period; it was also a year of bitter struggles by the out-of-work. Many of their leaders were arrested and imprisoned.

Hunger marchers greeted by police

The march reaching Hyde Park

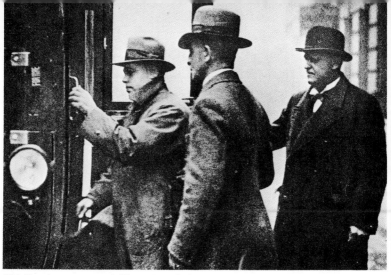

Wal Hannington arrested, November 1932

The government's policies were adding to the number of unemployed, and at the same time worsening their already desperate conditions. The means test was the cruellest of all their measures. In the years that followed the economic situation improved slightly and the government were able to make small concessions. Public opinion became more sympathetic to the unemployed. The national hunger march of 1936 was greeted in Hyde Park by a crowd estimated at two hundred and fifty thousand and an official reception from the London Trades Council.

To organize the great hunger marches collections had to be made to buy boots for the marchers, sleeping places arranged, and medical checks made to ensure that marchers were fit for the journey. At the same time the National Unemployed Workers' Movement continued its routine organizing among those on the dole queues. It was involved in such campaigns as extending the provision of cheap milk and free meals for under-nourished children. It continued to help members claim the relief that they were entitled to, and to demonstrate against Public Assistance Committees which interpreted the rules in the most rigid possible way.

In the last years before the war most of the activities of the NUWM were designed to keep the plight of the unemployed in the public eye. Unemployed workers invaded the gourmet dinners of the Wine and Food Society, and a banquet at which Sir John Anderson, the Minister of Labour, was being wined and dined by a group of employers. They hung banners with slogans drawing attention to the needs of the unemployed from public buildings, including the Monument in London.

The black coffin near Bow St Police Court

A black coffin, which had been carried through the streets of London on New Year's Eve, was delivered to 10 Downing Street as a symbol of the poverty of the unemployed. The furniture lorry carrying it was let through the police cordon which had earlier closed the street, suspicious that something was being planned.

The demonstrations and marches organized by the NUWM were far bigger and more militant than the Jarrow March, the one march which most people today have heard about and which for many people symbolizes the hungry thirties.

The strength and the strategy of the movement changed through the years in response to changes in the economic climate and the political strength of the working class, but throughout its existence it was a movement of audacity and determination.

NUWM demonstration, 1939

Its leaders took great personal risks, and many were imprisoned. Hannington went to prison ten times in the twenty years he spent in the NUWM. Tom Mann, veteran of the struggles of the late nineteenth century, became treasurer of the NUWM and he too was sent to prison as a result of speeches he made at their meetings.

The press, and even the official labour and trade union movement, tried to belittle the activities of the NUWM, tarring them with the Communist brush and accusing the hunger marchers of being organized from Moscow.

While the leading members of the movement were members of the Communist Party and made no secret of the fact, the influence of the NUWM spread far beyond the Party. Certainly it was committed to militant action and to changing a system which meant that millions of working class families faced poverty and near-starvation.

The Jarrow March was quite different in spirit. It was determinedly non-political. The agents of the three major political parties were involved in organizing it, and marchers were chosen to represent all sections of opinion. On the road, they went to church every Sunday. In spite of their striving after respectability, they too were denied recognition by the TUC and an audience from government ministers when they reached London.

Jarrow, on Tyneside, was a shipbuilding town, a town that depended not just on a single industry, but on a single firm — Palmers. Palmers' yard provided employment for most of Jarrow's workers, and Palmers controlled the town's council and endowed schools, libraries and hospitals when they could be persuaded that it was in their interest to do so.

When Palmers' yard closed, Jarrow became known as the town that was 'murdered'. Unemployment reached a staggering 80%, and the people of Jarrow decided to march to London to request special help.

Tyneside, 1976

Tyneside today is still an area of desolation. Unemployment runs at double the national average. New industries move in, but as in Merseyside they move out again when trade declines. Shipbuilding and repair are industries which respond very quickly to fluctuations in world trade, and so on Tyneside today there are still many families where parents and children stand side by side at the dole. Long-term unemployment is commonplace even among the skilled, in spite of the migration of many younger people to the midlands and the south in search of work. The closure of many pits in the Durham coalfield has increased unemployment. It is from Tyneside that this song comes:

When me father was a lad
Unemployment was so bad
He spent best part of his life down at the dole.
Straight from school to the labour queue
Raggy clothes and holey shoes
Combing pit-heaps for a manky bag o' coal.
And I'm standing at the door, at the same old bloody door,
Waiting for the pay-out like me father did before.

Nowadays we've got a craze
To follow clever Keynesian ways
And computers measure economic growth.
We've got experts milling round
Writing theories on the pound
Caring little whether we can buy a loaf.
And I'm standing at the door, at the same old bloody door,
Waiting for the pay-out like me father did before.

Alex Glasgow, from CLOSE THE COALHOUSE DOOR.

After the Second World War, employment levels were high; but the slow decline of the late sixties was followed by an accelerating slide in the mid-seventies. Even in times of so-called full employment, the unemployment figures for certain areas of the country — Tyneside, Merseyside, South Wales, Scotland and Northern Ireland — remained far above the national average.

Redundancy payments schemes reduced the militancy of resistance to redundancies as long as there was a reasonable prospect of finding another job, but as the unemployment figures rose and redundancy payments no longer compensated for loss of earnings resistance to sackings grew.

Redundancy in the motor industry, Birmingham, 1957

The work-in at Upper Clyde Shipbuilders in 1971 saved many of the 8,500 jobs that were threatened when the firm's five shipyards were declared bankrupt. The UCS shop stewards' committee decided on the work-in tactic largely as a propaganda exercise to demonstrate that the firm was still viable.

This was a time when unemployment among men in Scotland had risen by 40% a year. For workers all over the country the work-in made the demand for the right to work one that could be translated into action by those whose livelihoods were threatened by redundancy.

Sit-ins, work-ins and occupations followed in many parts of the country. Many of the occupations were led by small groups of militant workers prepared to chance their arms, but support quickly grew.

One of the stewards involved in the 1972 occupation at the Fisher-Bendix factory on Merseyside, part of the Thorns combine, describes the way in which they entered the boardroom. He tells how the board were discussing the projected closure of the plant when fourteen workers decided to go up there. More joined them until they were leading a growing crowd up the stairs. When they reached the top, they took the wrong turning and found themselves among the sparkling glass and silver of the executive dining room. The leaders had to push their way back through the crowd to find the boardroom door. They stopped outside, feeling an unexpected psychological barrier to entering, but at last two stewards at the front pushed each other in to face the assembled directors. The convenor told the directors that they had ten minutes to reconsider the closure plans.

When the directors announced that they could not reverse the decision they were given five minutes to leave.

The workers were then in possession of the factory and decided to continue the occupation. Every effort was made to keep all the workers involved in running the occupation, maintaining contacts with the Thorn combine organization and visiting other factories in the combine and in the area to gain support and the blacking of goods throughout the Thorns combine.

The settlement reached after the occupation was one of the best on Merseyside, and within a year Fisher Bendix had won a 35-hour week, a pound an hour and an extra week's holiday.

The effect on other factories in the Merseyside area was tremendous. In one stewards threatened, "We'll do a Fisher Bendix on you," and management withdrew redundancy notices.

Other occupations learned the lessons of the ones that had gone before. At a small barbed wire plant, Ainslie Wire, workers used their product to barricade themselves in and resist redundancy. They were also persuaded to use their occupation as a base from which to go out and seek support from other workers. Time and again it has been found that it is the degree of outside support from the labour movement which has determined the success of the occupation tactic.

Ainslie Wire factory occupation

Even where occupations have not finally succeeded in preventing redundancies, those taking part have found that the attempt to resist, the assertion of their right to work, has made the occupation worthwhile and has prepared them to fight future battles applying the lessons they have learned.

As the slump deepened and unemployment rose faster and faster, the individual struggles against redundancy became generalized into a national campaign. With a Labour government in power, however, the leaders of the trade union movement found themselves in an equivocal position. While they condemned unemployment as evil, appalling and shocking, they felt themselves so bound by their loyalty to the government and their involvement in it to consent to policies which put more people out of work. While Jack Jones, the leader of the TGWU called for a shorter working week to provide more jobs, he showed no intention of entering any fight for it or backing his members if they followed his call.

In 1975 a demonstration against unemployment and a lobby of Parliament were called by the North West Region of the TUC for November 26th. The call was backed by trade unionists up and down the country, principally the North London (No. 8) area of the Confederation of Shipbuilding and Engineering Unions, the London Cooperative Party, and the Rank and File Organising Committee. The TUC disowned the protest, fearing that it might have 'an anti-government nature', and Len Murray, the general secretary, circulated Trades Councils and member unions calling on them not to support it. In spite of this intervention, the protest went ahead and more than 20,000 workers marched from Euston Station to the House of Commons, passing Congress House, the TUC headquarters, on the way.

Out of the success of this march grew a campaign for the Right to Work, sponsored by the Rank and File Organising Committee. Plans were made for a march of unemployed workers from Manchester to London. Support for the march was sought from trade union branches, shop stewards committees and trades councils throughout the country. While more than a thousand trade union bodies gave support or affiliated to the campaign, others refused to do so because it was not recognized by the official labour and trade union movement.

The eighty marchers spent three weeks on the road, using the march as one of them put it as an 'anger march, not a hunger march'. As in the unemployed movement of the thirties, there were in the right to work campaign many unemployed workers with experience of organizing in industry. They applied this experience to their campaign. The march acted as a flying picket, holding meetings at factory gates or inside the factories themselves along their route.

On the first day the marchers were led by two veterans of past hunger marches — Harry McShane and Joe Ford who had marched from Manchester three times in the 1930s. The marchers left the road soon after the start of the march to go onto a building site where two workers from a contracting firm were working overtime to dismantle a crane, in spite of the fact that electricians on the site were on strike. The building workers agreed to leave the crane in place.

At Rugeley in Staffordshire marchers joined strikers on the picket line outside the Colourtrend factory, where management were refusing to allow a group of workers to transfer from one union to another although both unions agreed to the change.

At Clay Cross the council gave the marchers a civic reception, and the next morning breakfast was cooked by some of the banned ex-councillors.

The Yorkshire area of the miners' union was among the trade union bodies sponsoring the march, so all through Yorkshire the marchers were welcomed in the miners' welfare clubs.

Meetings and other activities punctuated the march as it passed through the midlands. In Coventry a delegation from the Chrysler, Stoke, factory came out onto the road to meet them and the Chrysler Shop Stewards' Committee banner was carried with the march to London. The Chrysler workers had very recently been involved in their own fight for the right to work. Their banner went with the marchers into the Triumph factory where they proclaimed their opposition to overtime being worked while redundant car workers lined up at the dole.

At the Austin factory at Longbridge, Birmingham, marchers went into the canteen explaining to the workers why they were marching and gaining their support.

In Birmingham they invaded the New Street Station, leafletting passengers and railway workers in support of the NUR's opposition to rail cuts.

Just as in 1932 police drew their batons on unemployed marchers in the Edgware Road, so they did again in 1976, this time further up the road. When the marchers reached Staples Corner, where the Edgware Road intersects the North Circular, several deputations had left the march to visit factories in North West London. The remaining marchers and a number of local trade unionists who had joined them for the final stage went up to speak to construction workers on the uncompleted Staples Corner flyover. As they came back into the main road, a policeman seized the lead banner and other police attacked the marchers.

Three more attacks followed, one outside the Hendon police station, where more police were waiting in nearby side streets. Some of them had come from Brixton at the opposite side of London. The next two attacks were outside Smiths Industries factory where one of the marchers had been a steward. More police, including members of the armed Special Patrol Group, arrived by coach to join in the affray, while a police helicopter hovered overhead. The independent trade union committee of inquiry set up by Barnet Trades Council to investigate the incident concluded:

"The committee had evidence which it accepts from marchers and independent observers of excessive and indiscriminate violence by the police during all these incidents and also in the police station.

There was also evidence of injuries to the police and of marchers fighting back. But this does not excuse
— Dragging people by the hair
— Throwing a national newspaper reporter's notebook over a police van
— Beating up an unconscious man
— Telling a marcher, 'Why don't you fuck off to Russia?'
— Indiscriminate use of truncheons
— Kneeing a marcher in the groin and delivering a karate chop to his neck
— Jumping on a man's stomach in the police station
— Telling a marcher in the police station to get on his knees and crawl to the cell."

More than 60 marchers were injured, some needing hospital treatment. Two suffered internal bleeding. Forty-three were arrested on charges which ranged from obstruction through assault to grievous bodily harm.

One of the marchers, Danny Evaristo, the former chairman of Greenwich Trades Council, was told by the doctor in the police station that he hadn't been injured — the doctor couldn't see any red marks on his skin, he said. Danny is black.

Harry McShane speaking at the Albert Hall

A week after the rally which filled the Albert Hall at the end of the Right to Work March, there was an assembly at the Central Hall Westminster. The initiative for organizing this was taken by the London Cooperative Political Committee and the North London engineers. Although the TUC withheld its approval, the assembly commanded widespread support and brought together delegates from many hundreds of trade union organizations who pledged themselves to continue the fight against unemployment.

Dennis Skinner, M.P. for the Clay Cross area, speaking at the Central Hall

One of the strongest demonstrations against unemployment and the cuts in public services was held in Dundee, where in March 1976 50,000 workers came out on strike for an afternoon.

All over the country action is being taken against the worsening situation. There are campaigns against hospital closures and against education cuts, and strikes by transport workers against cuts in services.

In many factories workers opposed redundancies and were backed by trades councils who organized marches against unemployment and cuts.

In Dundee in August 1976 parents and children occupied a new nursery school which had been built and then left empty. They used the occupation as a base for a campaign for more nursery education.

In many parts of the country unemployed workers have occupied Job Centres as a protest against their failure to offer work. They have also occupied empty properties to provide places where the unemployed can meet and organize.

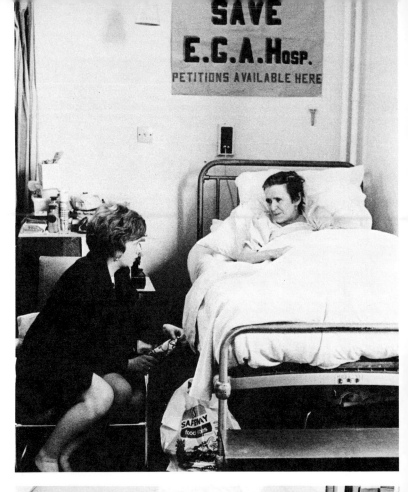

Protests were made on several occasions when banquets were held at public expense. On one such occasion Len Murray, the TUC general secretary, was being entertained by a group of employers in the Black Country. Unemployed workers picketed the hall. As Len Murray arrived, one of them moved forward to put a sticker on his car demanding the right to work. Police prevented him. Just then a waiter pushed up a trolley with the soup for the dinner on it, so the sticker was stuck on there instead. The waiter read it, took it off and slowly went up to Len Murray's car. He stuck it on, saying, "That's where that belongs."

In September 1976, nearly 600 unemployed, many recent school leavers, marched from London to Brighton where the Trades Union Congress was meeting, and joined a massive lobby organized by the National Union of Public Employees against the cuts in public services.

In the thirties Hannington had seen that the threat of fascism was one against which the unemployed must be organized with the employed. He wrote:

"Unless the unemployed are organized under the leadership of the working class movement there is always the danger of their becoming the pawns of Fascist adventurers."

The mounting racialism evident today makes it clear that it is as vital as ever that the fight against racism is seen as part and parcel of the fight for the right to work.

The campaign continues as unemployment grows. Unemployment will remain a central political issue so long as capitalism survives. No way has been found to regulate the cycle of booms and slumps, and the system can only attempt to solve its problems by choosing between the evils of unemployment and inflation.

The details of what has been meant by the demand for the right to work have changed since it was first posed, but at all times those who have raised the demand have made it plain that they refuse to see human beings regarded as disposable assets, to be treated in the same way as machines in the calculations of the capitalists.

The fight cannot be left to the trade union leaders who are paralysed by their loyalty to the Labour government while the government in turn dedicates its energies to making industry profitable on the terms laid down by the international bankers. The unemployed cannot fight alone, since by losing their jobs they have lost their power at the point of production. Therefore the fight must be carried on by rank-and-file workers uniting with the unemployed. It is left to the rank and file to put pressure on their leaders to transform their verbal opposition to unemployment into action, but if their pressure fails, it is the rank and file who must take the decision to act independently of these leaders.

Battles have been won by the rank and file in the fight for the right to work, and many more can and will be won in the future. The state has recognized its responsibility to keep unemployed and their dependents from starvation. The eight-hour day has been won in most industries. Battles have been won against overtime and to protect manning levels, but these are only limited victories. If every worker had the right to a job, it would be necessary for the workers to be in control of the resources of production and the social services. This would undermine the whole basis of the system. Therefore, the fight for the right to work is essentially a fight against the system of capital — within which workers are simply another commodity.

Marx wrote:

> "... behind the right to work stands power over capital, behind power over capital, the appropriation of the means of production ... the abolition of wage labour, capital and their mutual relationship."

Or, to use the words of the last verse of the song 'The Wild Colonial Boy':

> "The moral of this story, the moral of this song,
> Is simply that to rise and fight, cannot be seen as wrong
> For wherever there are classes, there the rich and poor will be
> And the workers gathered here today, must fight for liberty."

Further Reading

Historical background

General

A.L. Morton, *A People's History of England*
E.P. Thomson, *The Making of the English Working Class (1780-1832)*

19th Century

Novels by such authors as Mrs. Gaskell, George Eliot, Dickens
Karl Marx and Frederick Engels, *The Manifesto of the Communist Party*

Early 20th century

K. D. Brown, *Labour and Unemployment 1900-1910*

The 1930s

Noreen Branson and Margot Heinemann, *Britain in the Nineteen Thirties*, Panther
Wal Hannington, *Unemployed Struggles 1919-1939*, Gollancz and E.P. Publishers Ltd, *Depressed Areas*, Left Book Club, *Black Coffins of the Unemployed*
Harry McShane's autobiography, Pluto Press, 1977
Walter Greenwood, *Love on the Dole*, Cape and Penguin
George Orwell, *The Road to Wigan Pier*, Secker & Warburg and Penguin
H.L. Beales & R.S. Lambert (ed), *Memoirs of the Unemployed*, E.P. Publishing Ltd.
Ellen Wilkinson, *The Town that was Murdered*, Gollancz — the story of Jarrow and the Jarrow March by the town's M.P.
Alan Plater, Alex Glasgow & Sid Chaplin, *Close the Coalhouse Door*, Methuen a play from Tyneside.
Autobiographies which contain memories of the thirties include Archie Hill, *Summer's End*, and Will Paynter, *My Generation*
Bertolt Brecht, *Selected Poems*, trans. H.R. Hays, Methuen

Present day background

Child Poverty Action Group, *Unemployment*, a special issue of their magazine Poverty, Autumn 1975

John Deason, *Fight for the Right to Work, No Return to the Thirties,*
a Right to Work Campaign pamphlet
Counter Information Services, Crisis Reports: *Unemployment, Who's
Next for the Chop, Cutting the Welfare State (Who Profits?),
Women Under Attack, Racism (Who Profits?)*
Patrick Kinnersley, *Hazards of Work and How to Fight Them,* Pluto Press,
on the effects of overtime and shift-work on workers' health
Tom Clarke, *Sit-in at Fisher Bendix,* IWC pamphlet
Willie Thompson and Finlay Hart, *The UCS Work-in,* Lawrence & Wishart

Acknowledgements

Acknowledgements are due to those who have allowed us to quote from
copyright sources:

Harcourt Brace Jovanovich Inc. for the poem "Those Who Take the Meat
from the Table" from *Selected Poems of Bertolt Brecht*, trans. H.R. Hays.

Methuen & Co. for the poem "Close the Coalhouse Door" by Alan
Plater, based on short stories by Sid Chaplin with songs by Alex Glasgow.

Alex Glasgow for the song "My Granny Tells Me" from the record *Songs
of Alex Glasgow,* produced by Mawson & Wareham Music Ltd .

Independent Labour Party for the poem "Eat More" by Joe Corrie from
Rebel Songs

Jonathan Cape and the Estate of Walter Greenwood for the extract from
Love on the Dole

E.P. Publishing Ltd. for the extract from *Unemployed Struggles* by
Wal Hannington

Acknowledgements and thanks are also due to the following for permission
to use their pictures: The Radio Times Hulton Picture Library for pages
17 top, 74, 84-5, 91, 96-8, 100, 103-05, 107, 108, 111; The Mary Evans
Picture Library for pages 82, 93, 95; the Illustrated London News Picture
Library for pages 39, 94, 106; Socialist Worker for page 123, Angela
Phillips for page 122; and John Sturrock (Report) for page 113